LORD, WHEN?

A BIBLICAL PERSPECTIVE OF THE SECOND COMING

D1598495

JOHN J. COBB

ISBN 978-1-63885-024-3 (Paperback)
ISBN 978-1-63885-025-0 (Digital)

Quotations from the Holy Bible: King James Version (KJV) copyright 1989 by Thomas Nelson, Inc., Nashville, Tennessee. Cover artwork title "Destruction in Nature" by Pat Marvenko Smith ©1982, 1992 have been used by permission. For information on the artwork go to www.revelationillustrated.com

Covenant Books, Inc.
11661 Hwy 707
Murrells Inlet, SC 29576
www.covenantbooks.com

CONTENTS

PREFACE

I hope this book will not be just another one on the end-times. Instead, I hope it will awaken and stir the hearts and souls of Christians to once again develop a deeper love for the study of eschatology. I do not believe in date setting and will not put such an idea forward within the pages of this book. However, I will present as clear and concise a picture as possible about the time frame referred to as the Seventieth Week of Daniel (Daniel 9:20–27). This period of time affirms that God has decreed a specific time frame for His chosen nation Israel and the world. The Bible also affirms this period consists of seven years and seventy-five days and culminates the history of mankind.

Since the Bible is the major support for much of what's written in this book, I do not want the reader to become bogged down in trying to figure out which book of the Bible is being referred to. Therefore, I have intentionally chosen to forego the use of abbreviation when referencing portions of Scripture. This should make it easier for Christians and all who read this book to search "the Scriptures…to find out whether these things" are so (Acts 17:11b).

Finally, I believe my generation will probably not witness the return of Jesus Christ, but will be with Him when He returns. I am not being dogmatic, nor am I setting dates since only the three Persons of the Trinity know when Christ will return. However, my understanding of prophecy and the signs of the times support my conclusions. Therefore, I'm dedicating this book to our children and their children. I believe they will witness the rise of the antichrist, the revived Roman Empire, and ultimately, all those things recorded in the book of Revelation that will lead up to the Second Coming.

ACKNOWLEDGMENTS

My wife, Fay Cobb, Loretta Hinton, Bettye Johnson (Deceased), Ron Grace, Linda Dailey, and my pastor Walstone E. Francis (Deceased), whose words of inspiration, wisdom and encouragement became the motivating factor for completing this work.

INTRODUCTION

Except for predestination and its associated doctrines of election, foreknowledge, calling, and God's decrees, there is no greater subject that divides the Body of Christ as does the Rapture. Does it take place before, at the midway point, or at the end of the Tribulation period? These questions are at the forefront of this important doctrine of the Christian faith.

Many have written books on the subject exploring all views: Pre-Tribulation, Mid-Tribulation, Post-Tribulation, and the latest view—the Pre-Wrath. Although they all provide invaluable information about the Second Coming, many are still asking, "What shall be the sign of thy coming, and the end of the world?" (Matthew 24:3).

As the signs of His coming become more obvious, Christians are becoming increasingly aware that the Second Coming must be near. Because it is such an important part of our faith, it is inconceivable that our Lord would leave us in the dark. Passages such as those given in Paul's letters to the Thessalonians, the gospel of Matthew, and the book of Titus support this conclusion. All these passages encourage us to "live soberly, righteously, and godly, in this present world; looking for that blessed hope, and the glorious appearing of the great God and our Savior Jesus Christ" (Titus 2:13). It would seem from these and other passages that God's desire is that our lives be characterized by holiness and self-discipline as we await the return of our Savior.

It is interesting that Paul calls this our "blessed hope" and not simply hope. I believe his reasoning for doing so was to further stress the happiness and joy that will be ours at the Second Coming. It is more than just hoping and waiting for the event (which is important), it is the final fulfillment of God's promises to us. It is our glorification, the perfect unity and fellowship of the saints, freedom from the presence of sin and into the company of the angelic host. These are good reasons for looking forward to the Second Coming.

However, this writer does not think that Paul just had those things in mind when he called the Second Coming "blessed." The way he ends this wonderful verse supports this conclusion. Notice what he says: "And the glorious appearing of the great God and our Savior Jesus Christ." What makes this event far above any hope that we can imagine is our Blessed Lord and Savior's appearance. We will see Him as He is and will be with Him forever. He is the object of our blessed hope, and it is our faith in all that He has promised that keeps us longing for that day.

Apart from the regenerative experience, the first resurrection (and the blessings associated with it) is undoubtedly the greatest thing that can ever happen to a person. As such, there must be a reasonable amount of surety about certain facts. For example, if the Tribulation does precede the Rapture, what impact will it have on one's faith? What will be the response once the stark realization come that either I've been left behind or the Rapture does occur after the Tribulation. This will undoubtedly have an effect on one's faith and, subsequently, one's hope. These are serious questions that need to be at least considered and pondered by every believer.

At the heart of Paul's teaching to the church at Corinth was the truth that extreme care must be taken on how we build on the foundation that he and the other apostles had laid (1 Corinthians 3:10; cf. Ephesians 2:20–22). He had in mind the teachings of and about Jesus Christ. He is the foundation of all Christian doctrine. Teachings built on any other foundation is spiritually worthless in helping saints to know God and His will. Whether we're talking about the Trinity, original sin, justification by faith alone, election, sanctification, regeneration or any other essential doctrine of our faith, the commonality among them all is the centrality of Christ. Therefore, it is the responsibility of every Christian to have scriptural knowledge not only of the doctrines named earlier, but eschatology (teaching of last things or Second Coming) as well.

Finally, the notion or belief that it does not matter what one believes about the Second Coming is to ignore God's clear revelation in His word about it. It further ignores the Holy Spirit's declaration that "all Scripture is given by inspiration of God, and is profitable for doctrine, for reproof, for correction in righteousness: that the man of God may be perfect, thoroughly furnished unto all good works" (2 Timothy 3:16–17). By implication, this means the doctrine of eschatology should receive as much attention as the other teachings of the Bible. Moreover, how can one talk seriously about justification without glorification, or how can one discuss glorification with any seriousness without first exploring the truths presented in eschatology? The Bible does not do so, and neither should we.

CHAPTER 1

THE QUESTION

Tell us when shall these things be? and what shall be the
sign of thy coming, and of the end of the world?
—Matthew 24:3

There are perhaps no questions more important about the Second Coming than those put to our Lord in the Olivet Discourse. I thank God that the Holy Spirit moved the disciples to ask such relevant questions, not only for their time, but ours as well. In making such a statement, I do not imply, nor do I mean that other passages of Scripture written on this subject are not just as important. Such a statement would not only be irresponsible, but a denial that God inspired "all" Scripture. Therefore, the same principles employed in exegeting other doctrines of our faith must be applied just as vigorous, if not more so, when it comes to this particular area. In doing so, we not only protect the integrity and validity of Scripture; but also answer the skeptics who continually insist the Bible is not inspired, inerrant, and infallible.

The truth that a deliverer would come, be crucified, buried, and resurrected is revealed first in the Old Testament (Genesis 3:15; Psalm 22; Isaiah 53). Even the resurrection of the saints is a doctrine first seen, or at least implied in Abraham's faith that God would raise his son from the dead if he offered him as a sacrifice (Romans 4:20–21; Hebrews 11:19). But even if Abraham's faith does not suggest he believed in the resurrection, we can look to the books of Job and Daniel, where both prophets talks about it (Job 19:26–27; Daniel 12:1–2). However, God's revelation to them was incomplete and incomprehensible not only to the writers, but the people of that era as well (cf. Daniel 12:9; 1 Peter. 1:10–12). For example, the Lord's prophecy that at the close of the great tribulation, the angels will gather the elect from the four corners of the world. Can you imagine the confusion, misinformation, and false teaching that would abound if this was all that Scripture provided about this part of the Second Coming? We would not know that every Christian would be translated and possess the same body we had when we were alive (Job 19:26). We would not know that our physical bodies would be transformed from one that is corruptible and limited by the laws of nature to one incorruptible, immortal, and glorious (1 Corinthians 15:51–53). Nor would we know there would be a specific order regarding the Rapture and the glorification of the saints. First, the bodies of Christians who died before the Second Coming will be raised, reunited with their spirit, and "caught up" or raptured first (1 Thessalonians 4:15–17). After this happens, those of us who are alive will follow and be joined with them and our Lord forever. "All this" says Paul, "will happen in the twinkling of an eye" (1 Corinthians 15:52). These facts were mysteries to the Church until the point when Paul wrote his letters to the Churches at Thessalonica and Corinth. Both letters provide invaluable details about the order and transformation that this earthly body will undergo before being glorified.

So why do I place such importance on the twenty-fourth chapter of Matthew, especially in light of what's been said earlier? Unfortunately, some Christians give words written in red more credence and significance simply because our Savior spoke them. Although this is not my reasoning (as stated earlier, I believe wholeheartedly in both the verbal and plenary inspiration of Scripture), I do believe that it warrants special attention because it is one of the few times that our Lord spoke directly to this issue during His earthly ministry. Jesus provide many details about the events that surrounds and ushers in His Second Coming and the period of time known as the Tribulation and Great Tribulation. Though I do not want to be dogmatic, I will say that any study of eschatology would be incomplete without at least a cursory reading of our Lord's words recorded in the twenty-fourth chapter of Matthew.

When we examine this chapter in Matthew's gospel, we find two critical events being predicted—the destruction of the temple and the Second Coming. According to the Jewish Historian Josephus, Titus fulfilled the first of these two events during his siege of Jerusalem in AD 70. His account of the events that took place during this siege support our Lord's prediction more than thirty years earlier that the city would be surrounded and destroyed. Its destruction would be so complete, so thorough and final that there would not be left "one stone upon another."

But what does this have to do with the Second Coming? Like many others, I strongly believe that prophecy and world history centers around the nation Israel. Therefore, to fully understand the Second Coming, one's attention must be focused on events surrounding that nation. It is no accident the Jews did not fade into history and become simply a footnote in the annals of history as so many other nations. God's unconditional promise to Abraham fixed the certainty of that fact. When He declared to Abraham that He would one day give his descendants a land, it was dependent on His faithfulness and the character of His person. Though they would be disobedient, stray from Him, worship false gods and punished by Him, even to the extent of displacing them from their land, God will never go back on His promise to Abraham. Even after ignoring the warnings and urgings of His prophets and lastly rejecting and killing His Son, He remains faithful to His promises. No other people in the history of the human race can boast of such privileges and such powerful and wonderful promises as can the small nation of Israel.

To get a better idea of how all that's been said fit into the Olivet Discourse, we need to carefully examine the questions asked of Jesus by His disciples. They involved two specific areas of concerns. First, they wanted to know when "shall these things be?" This first question was in response to Jesus's comment about the temple, that "there shall not be left here one stone upon another, that shall not be thrown down" (Matthew 24:2 KJV).

Such a statement must have come as a shock to the disciples, especially because of the temple's magnificence and obvious solid construction. However, their response suggests they were neither puzzled nor amazed that such a thing could happen. They were eye-witnesses to the many miracles performed by the Master and therefore knew that whatever He said would come to pass.

In answer to their question, Jesus not only gave them the how and when but also "the who" of their question. Though Matthew records a good portion of this, it is Luke that provides greater details about how this would take place. Even though he does leave out the names of the people that would eventually destroy the temple and ultimately the city, it's not difficult to deduce the armies surrounding Jerusalem referred to in chapter twenty-one of Luke's gospel has to be that of Rome in AD 70. Even more graphic than that of Luke was the dismal picture painted by the Jewish historian Josephus. He wrote,

> Titus began the final assault on Jerusalem in the spring of AD 70. He had close to 100,000 soldiers facing a city with a population of at least 200,000, greatly augmented by a large number of pilgrims who were present at the Passover. The city was subjected to artillery that threw massive stones against the walls, and was surrounded by a huge mound to prevent escape. Those who tried to escape or terrorize the enemy were frequently captured and crucified—often 500 were nailed to crosses on a given day. The forests around Jerusalem were completely destroyed to supply the wood necessary for battering rams, ramps, catapults, camp fires, ladders, and the many crosses that rose outside the city (Wars of the Jews, V.x11.3).

This was only a portion of what went on in Jerusalem during that time. Scarcity of food not only led to starvation but also forced family members to turn against one another. Murder, robbery, and greed became the order of the day. All these things happened exactly as Jesus said they would. Yet this was not the end of the world, just a foretaste of what was to come, not just on the Jewish Nation but the entire world.

It was a devastating time for the Jews; not only did they lose their beloved city and temple, but their identity as a nation. They became a people without a country, scattered, and buried among the nations of the world. This was partial fulfillment of Ezekiel's prophecy recorded in the thirty-eighth chapter of his book. Though it was an accurate description of the Jewish people after the Roman seizure of Jerusalem, it was not a sign of their final fate. In God's eyes, they were still very much alive. This was the whole point behind Ezekiel's vision of the valley of dry bones—to give hope to the nation of Israel. The prophecy was God's way of telling His people that although they would stop being a nation, and would be scattered among the peoples of the world, they would never stop being His people. The focus was never on the burial, but the fact that one day, this same people would again become a sovereign nation and have her own land. She would by the Mighty Hand of God do what no other nation has ever done in the history of the human race—experience a resurrection.

In 1948, the second portion of that prophecy became a reality, as the tiny nation of Israel was recognized by the United Nations as a sovereign state. The importance of this event in prophecy must not stop at Israel becoming a nation once again; it goes further by reaffirming God's promise made to Abraham that His descendants would have all the land bordered by "the river of Egypt [the Niles] unto the great river, the river Euphrates" (Genesis 15:18), despite opposition from her enemies and the world. A casual glimpse of any map of the Middle East clearly shows that Israel still does not possess even a fraction of the land promised her by God through Abraham. What is also seen is that, when compared with her neighbors, she is much smaller.

This combined with the constant random acts of terrorism and the intensive hatred of her by the neighboring countries puts her in a precarious position. The increase pressure from western countries for Israel to give up even more of the little land she now holds to secure a Palestinian State further jeopardizes her safety and existence. However, despite these seemingly insurmountable odds, world leaders must understand and realize that no amount of peace summits, threats of war or acts of terror will ever displace this tiny nation again (Psalm 89:27–37). While opposition will continue to rise, each time God will prove His faithfulness by outstretching His mighty hand against the enemies of the peoples He refers to as "the apple of His eye" (Deuteronomy 32:10).

Second, the disciples wanted to know what signs would precede His coming. The Jews more than anyone understood the significance of signs. They knew that signs and miracles would authenticate the true Messiah. This single fact is the main reason some find the Jews' rejection of Jesus so difficult to understand. After all, they had many advantages that were unavailable to the Gentiles, especially as it related to the prophets who foretold of the Messiah's coming (Isaiah 53:2–3, 7–8). They had much to boast of about the person of Christ, because it was to and through them and only them that He would come. Also, as the Apostle Paul points out in his letter to the Roman Christians, God had entrusted His Holy word and law to them. Except for Luke, Jewish writers wrote every other book in the New Testament. They had waited for centuries for that glorious day when their messiah would come and release them from their oppressors. They longed for the day when their king would usher in a time of peace and prosperity akin to David's reign. Yet, when their king finally did come, not only did they fail to recognize or want Him, these same people, though indirectly, crucified Him.

How could such an obvious mistake in identity be made, especially in light of everything Jesus did? The Scriptures clearly revealed that everything He did authenticated him as being the promised Messiah. Perhaps the best answer to such a perplexing question was the one given by Jesus after His disciples asked Him why He spoke in parables. His answer, recorded in the thirteenth chapter of Matthew, is interesting and shed much light about why the Jews missed the first appearance of their long-awaited Messiah. Notice what He said: "it is given unto you to know the mysteries of the kingdom of heaven, but to them it is not given…Therefore speak I to them in parables: because they seeing, see not; and hearing, they hear not; neither do they understand. And in them is fulfilled the prophecy of Esaias, which saith, 'By hearing ye shall hear, and shall not understand; and seeing ye shall see, and shall not perceive" (Matthew 13:11–14 KJV).

Based on this response, Jesus spoke as He did to fulfill prophecy. Scripture is clear that if He had not provided private interpretation to His disciples (and lastly to us through the Holy Spirit), they would have remained ignorant to their meaning and significance. This, I might add, is true of all scripture. That is, without the Holy Spirit's illumination, we would be just as blind as they were and would reject the Savior as all unbelievers do today. Therefore, we should not and must never look down on the Jews because of their failure to recognize their Messiah. Boasting on our part is not only dangerous, but also arrogant and does not reflect a true understanding of God's love, grace, and mercy toward them.

In the eleventh chapter of Romans, Paul expounds further on this matter by exhorting Christians that he "would not, brethren, that ye should be ignorant in this mystery (lest ye should be wise in your own conceits) that blindness in part is happened to Israel until the fullness of the Gentiles be come in" (Romans 11:25 KJV). This passage points out the blindness of the Jews was part of God's eternal plan of election and has nothing to do with our being more deserving of His salvation than they. What He has done, He has done by His own sovereign choice and purpose. Meanwhile, the Jews will remain blinded until He completes His plan for the Gentiles. The world and some Christians may consider this unrealistic or unfair. However, it does not alter the fact that in eternity, the Godhead took steps to make certain the calling and salvation of those elected before the foundation of the world.

As stated earlier, the Jews clearly understood the importance of signs, not just because they were Jews, but because of every day experiences. This is not unique to them only, since all of us use signs to a certain extent. For example, when we're driving, signs let us know that we're on the right road to our destination and warn us of danger. The person that can read and understand signs are aware of where they've been, where they are, and where they're going. This is the reason the disciples asked about the signs that would point to the Second Coming. They wanted to be able to discern and understand the times, seasons, and events of their world.

However, before Jesus answered the disciples' question, He prefaced it with the warning that although they would see the signs, they were to "take heed" of them. In other words, they must pay particular and careful attention about how they understood them as they unfolded. Jesus stressed that signs are important, but if that's all we're looking for, the possibility of deception or misinterpretation increases considerably. We must not only be able to recognize the signs; we must also depend on the Holy Spirit's illumination of them. There is nothing worse than looking at a sign where a letter is missing, defaced, or covered. It is our Master's desire that we not only know the signs, but that we are able to discern them. His reasoning for this is that there will be those who would either intentionally or unintentionally use them to deceive us.

After this stern warning, Jesus began to lay out before the disciples the signs that would usher in His return. There would be wars and rumors of wars, famines, pestilences, and earthquake in different places. These are all signs that point, alert, and let Christians know the end is near. They are not the ends in and of themselves any more than a signpost on the road is the destination that it points to. All these signs must and shall occur before our Lord's return.

Although many would apply these signs mostly to Israel, I believe they are more directly related to the Church. Although Matthew wrote his gospel to a Jewish audience with the specific purpose of authenticating Jesus as the Son of David, it still must be understood and seen as a book written mainly to Christians. Therefore, the prophecies given in the twenty-fourth chapter, as well as other passages, are mainly for the benefit of Christians, and not Jews.

When one looks at the events depicted in verses five through eight of the twenty-fourth chapter of Matthew, one cannot help but see their similarity to the behavior and character of today's society. These verses also add support to the conclusion that Jesus's warning was directed at His future Church. False teachers with their deception would intensify as His Second Coming draws near. Further examination of the verses in this chapter clearly points to a time when Christians would be the focus of the world's hatred. The people of the world will seek to destroy us and believe that they're doing the work of God. The Jews could hardly be the targets of such persecution, since Jesus says of these people in that verse that they are hated "for my namesake." They are being persecuted because of the Person represented by the name "Jesus." Undoubtedly, Jesus had in mind those who love and trust Him as their Lord and Savior. Based on this, it is unimaginable that any unconverted Jew would willingly die for the namesake of one they regard as an impostor and blasphemer.

Further signs point out that men will become worse and worse, false prophets will increase, arising and deceiving many. In His continued account of the last days, Jesus explains the love of man will wax cold (Matthews 24:12; cf. 2 Timothy 3:13). The Greek word translated "wax" in that passage describes a chilling kind of love. It is a chill that comes from water slowly being frozen over a long period of time. The callousness and pure evil portrayed by human beings today toward one another is just that kind of coldness. No longer is a reason needed to hurt or kill today; it's done now for the most trivial reasons. This is the idea behind the Greek word for "wax." Men will get worse and worse, not necessarily because they want to, but because they can't help it. It is the outward expression of man's depravity and sinfulness in a totally unbridled state. This verse in Matthew, as well as the passage in Second Timothy (2 Timothy 3:13), should put to rest this idea the world will eventually get better as time goes on. There is only one hope for man and that is the saving power of Jesus Christ.

Jesus continues by stressing that following these signs will be "great tribulations, such as was not since the beginning of the world to this time, no, nor ever shall be. And except those days should be shortened, there should no flesh be saved" (Matthews 24:21–22 KJV). This statement alone let us know that times are going to get worse, not better. The only reason God will shorten that time is due solely to His love for the elect.

Arguments exist on whether the elect spoken of here is Israel or the Church. Based on this term's normal use in the New Testament and the context surrounding its use in chapter twenty-four, it would seem that Jesus has the Church in mind and not Israel. This becomes more obvious when we look at the fact that both Old and New Testaments are in fact one covenant. Unlike the Old Testament, the New Testament does not have Israel as its primary focus. While it is true that nearly all of its authors are Jewish, the New Testament presents Christ as Redeemer and Savior to all people—Jew and Gentile alike.

Israel was and remains the elect and chosen nation of God, this can and never will change (cf. Psalm 89:29–37). However, according to Scripture, Christians were "chosen…in him, before the foundation of the world," (Ephesians 1:4 KJV) which suggests the Church was God's elect way before the nation of Israel. The nation of Israel was a picture or type of the Church in the Old Testament and was given specific promises unique to her, and therefore irrevocable. She was God's elect nation and enjoys the unique blessings that go with that election. But again, even this election is typical of the greater election; that of being elected into the spiritual nation, which the physical nation was only a type or shadow. Therefore, to apply this term to Israel in the New Testament would be to mingle the type with its reality.

There is perhaps no other book in the entire Bible that sheds more light on the importance of shadows and types, as does the letter to the Hebrews. The writer shed light on this truth by putting into perspective the purposes of the symbols, types, and shadows in the Old Testament. He does so by drawing a contrast between the imperfection of Moses, the Prophets, the Aaronic Priesthood, Tabernacle, and blood sacrifices. As symbols, they were not in and of themselves "the end," they only pointed to the objective truths they portrayed. In a sense, shadows are the physical pictures of spiritual truths. Therefore, to understand the various facets of salvation, including our election, there must be some understanding of the Old Testament.

In conclusion, we would do well to heed the words of our Master about understanding the signs of the times and their relevancy to His return, "Now learn the parable of the fig-tree; When his branch is yet tender, and putteth forth leaves, ye know that summer is nigh: So likewise ye, when ye shall see all these things, know that it is near, even at the doors" (Matthews 24:32–33 KJV). How close is our Master's return? No one knows, but the signs clearly suggest the leaves are slowly protruding from the bud. How long? Not long. As the late songwriter Andréa Crouch puts it,

> Count the years as months; count the months as days,
> Any day now, we'll be going home.

CHAPTER 2

THE NEXT GREAT SIGN

And what shall be the sign of thy coming,
and of the end of the world?

—Matthew 24:3

"MILLIONS OF PEOPLE DISAPPEARING, PLANES CRASHING, MAS-SIVE TRAFFIC ACCIDENTS!" Are these future headlines that will flood the airwaves and printed media after the Rapture? After the church is raptured, will the world be thrown into chaos and hysteria? Many Christians are convinced that this is indeed an accurate scenario of the Rapture and the events that follow. Passages such as Revelation 3:10 and 1 Thessalonians 5:9 and 4:14 appear to support this view. However, when placed alongside all other scriptures about the Second Coming, this view comes up short in this writer's opinion.

As stated in the previous chapter, Jesus stressed His return would not take place until all those events spoken of in verses four through fourteen of Matthew twenty-four had occurred. The failure of some Christians to take heed of this one fact is the main reason so many are accepting the teaching that the Second Coming is immi-nent. They failed the test of the Bereans (Acts 17:11) by not testing the teachings of preachers and teachers against Holy Scripture—the final arbiter of God's truth.

However, such a misunderstanding of God's word in this area is nothing new. Its first instance was more than two thousand years ago in the little church at Thessalonica. They, too, had obviously fallen victims to false teachings about the Second Coming.

Before I go on, I do need to stress that the term "false teachers" in this section is restricted to its use in the Thessalonians' passages under discussion in this chapter. I am in no way inferring that those who teach a view other than "post-Tribulation" are false teachers, since many of these godly men I highly esteem and have the utmost respect. However, I do believe that to arrive at the conclusion that Scripture lean more toward a pre-Tribulation Rapture than any other view requires more eisegesis (interpreting a text from one's own pre-suppositions, ideas, or biases) than exegesis (interpreting a passage by examining Scripture through critical examination and interpretation). Again, this is my personal belief arrived at through much study, the Spirit's illumination, prayer, and studies from other godly men and, therefore, is by no means a dogmatic statement on my part.

Having said that, let us return to the matter under discussion. Seemingly after Paul had founded the church at Thessalonica, false teachers had crept in and distorted his teaching about the Day of the Lord. The Thessalonian Christians' blind acceptance of their teaching resulted from their claim they were speaking through the spirit of prophecy. Letters circulated by false teachers supporting this new doctrine and crediting them as being from Paul added to the problem. Unaware that he had not commissioned them, and the fact they were not speaking by the authority of the Holy Spirit was another reason for the Thessalonians failure to discern these false teachers' doctrines. The deception was so thorough that they had seemingly taken leave of their senses. Sound judgment and plain old common sense had clearly been thrown to the wind. Their faith had obviously become shaken and their minds troubled.

To fully appreciate the extent and condition they were in, we need to look closely at the term Paul used for *shaken*. The idea behind this word is the practice of sailors tying their ships to a pier during severe storms. Sometimes the wind and waves would forcibly tear them from the pier and drive them out into the sea. The reason for this was not because of any defect in the rope, nor was the rope holding the ship in a weakened state. The ship broke away because the rope was not securely tied to the pier. This was Paul's idea behind the word *shaken*. The Thessalonians had become shaken from their faith because they were not properly grounded.

What an accurate picture of the Thessalonian Christians! Paul had taught them in this area previously (1 Thessalonians 5:1–2). They understood and accepted his teaching, and it became the grounds for their belief system in this area. However, because they had succumbed to false teaching that same foundation had crumbled. Like the ship earlier, their ropes had come loose from its foundation, and they found themselves in the stormy sea of confusion and anxiety. Their faith had been so badly shattered, so badly rattled, that some had stopped working. Their reasoning being that since the Lord's appearance was imminent, why become overly involved in world affairs. Later in the letter, Paul would firmly tell those who felt this way that if any man did not work, neither should he have the pleasure of eating (2 Thessalonians 3:10). However, he felt it necessary to deal with this critical problem about the Day of the Lord before he taught them on Christian living. Throughout his letters, you will find that this is always his pattern: teaching or doctrine first, followed by application.

Besides the teaching that the Second Coming was imminent, a second problem that had caused some confusion was Paul's teaching on the Lord coming as a thief in the night. Based on the fifth chapter of his first letter to this church, he must have already taught them about this issue. Otherwise, he would not have prefaced his argument with the statement "of the times and the seasons, brethren, ye have no need that I write unto you For yourselves know perfectly that the day of the Lord so cometh as a thief in the night" (1 Thessalonians 5:1 KJV). The Greek word he uses for *know* further supports this. It does not imply a cursory knowledge, but one that is thorough in its understanding. Somehow their understanding had become warped between the time that he had taught them about this issue and the occasion for his writing the letter. As a result, they were being lead to a wrong conclusion about how this truth was to be understood.

As an aside, I would add that this also shows the omniscience and love of God in that He inspired the apostle to pen these words to His church. He knew that both the Church of the first and twenty-first century would need it!

Having said that, let's briefly examine Paul's teaching in this area. First, he reminded them that the Lord will only catch those living in spiritual darkness by surprise when He returns. Spiritual darkness in the New Testament always has reference to the unsaved, since everything they do is done in darkness. The unsaved are obviously who Paul has in mind since Christians do not live in this state habitually. Their frame of mind is one that is against all that is godly, so even though the signs pointing to the Lord's return are clear and obvious, they will not be able to see them. However, this is not true of Christians because we are of the light. God has not hidden His truths about His Son's return from Christians but has revealed them to us in His Word. We should be fully aware of what's going on around us, especially as it relates to the Second Coming. The only reason that this day will catch some Christians by surprise is that they are not walking in the light and therefore are unable to judge the times and seasons.

This fact is important and cannot be overemphasized. If Christians know and understand the signs pointing to Christ's return, it will not catch them by surprise! On the other hand, the world will be, because of their blindness and hardness of heart. They see no need for looking up, no need or longing for the redemption of their mortal bodies. The world's concern will be to fulfill the lust of their mind and flesh. They are in darkness and blind to the goodness and mercy of God. If only they would realize the long-suffering of God is not a sign that He does not exist or that He overlook sin. Instead, it is a sign pointing them to His patience and loving-kindness toward sinners with the specific purpose of bringing them to repentance (Romans 2:4, cf. 2 Peter 3:9). In his hatred for God, man continues to harden his heart and as a result cannot see his own damnation.

Unfortunately, man see God's judgment in the same light and attitude as those in Noah's time who watched daily as he built the Ark. Every day, he warned them of the impending judgment of God, but they turned a deaf ear to his words. The flood subsequently destroyed them because they misjudged the signs and words of Noah. People today are making the same mistake. They ignore God's written and preached word and do not believe in the coming judgment of God.

There will be a second coming of our Lord and when He comes there will be no escape for those who have rejected Him. The prophet Amos gives us a vivid picture of the certainty of the coming destruction on the wickedness of this world as well as on those who might foolishly think they will escape by their cleverness. The futility of such an assumption is as "though a man fled from a lion only to meet a bear, as though he entered his house and rested his hand on the wall only to have a snake bite it" (Amos 5:19 KJV). Even though men will cry for the rocks to fall on them and to be hidden from God's wrath, it will be a cry that will go unheard. If you have not accepted the Lord Jesus Christ as your Savior, now is the time; do not wait until that day comes on the world because it will be too late.

In the fifteenth chapter of Revelation, an angel declares the temple in heaven was filled with smoke. No one was able to enter it until God's wrath had been fully poured out upon the world (Revelation 15:8). God's wrath will be meted out upon the world in its full strength during this time. On the other hand, as children of the light, we must see and understand the mysteries of God through the eyes of the Holy Spirit. Only He knows the deep things of God and desires to reveal them to us. Even though we have not been given the entire picture, we can still be certain of the nearness of His coming. If we look to the Holy Spirit, He will explain God's Word that speaks about the signs around us. By understanding their significance, we can better prepare ourselves spiritually for that blessed day and the terrible tribulation and judgment that will usher in our Lord's return.

In a sense, most Christians of today have become like those in Thessalonica. In misunderstanding the teaching about Christ coming as a thief in the night, many have blindly accepted the idea of an imminent return of Christ, despite clear teaching in God's word to the contrary. Although I believe strongly that no man knows the day or hour of our Lord's return, we can know the season. It is God's will and desire that we be prepared for the Second Coming. As stated earlier, it is inconceivable that He would leave us uninformed about such an important event, especially since the Bible refers to it as the Christian's blessed hope. God expects us to be watchful, sober and ready for His Son's return. Therefore, let us be as the Bereans, not only ready to receive God's Word, but diligently searching "the Scriptures daily to find out whether these things were so" (Acts 17:11 KJV).

CHAPTER 3

THE EVENTS LEADING TO CHRIST'S RETURN

For that day shall not come.

—2 Thessalonians 2:3

Not only were the Christians at Thessalonica confused about the Lord coming as a thief in the night, they were also unclear about specific events that will precede the Rapture. Some believe this was the result of a misinterpretation of an earlier letter sent by Paul. However, a more likely explanation is they were led astray by the same false teachers spoken of earlier. In either case, they had become unsettled and worried about this particular issue and needed clarification. Added to this was the concern that those who had already died would miss the glorious return of the Lord Jesus Christ. Because this touched each believer in a personal way, Paul devoted almost all of chapter four of his first letter to the Thessalonians in explaining this teaching. He closed that chapter by stressing that those who had died in Christ would be raptured and receive their glorified bodies first.

However, before the glorification and rapture of the saints can happen, two major events must take place. First, there has to be a great falling away from the Christian faith. Although we are not given the specific reason for it, we can surmise that it probably has ties to the terror that will be unleashed on the church and the world during the tribulation period by the antichrist. The world under his leadership will show itself in acts of hatred against Christians (as well as those who pose a threat to him either directly or indirectly), in a manner that will be unparalleled in the history of mankind. This will be in fulfillment of our Lord's prophecy that "ye will be hated by all nation" (Matthew 24:9).

Unlike today where Christians can escape to a country where religious freedom is possible, during this time, there will be no haven of safety. This period will indeed be times of great tribulation. Some may try to soften this truth by again applying the "ye" in the passage above to Israel instead of the Church. However, a look at Jewish history and their failure to recognize and accept Jesus as their Messiah refutes such a view. Additional support that the Church is in view here is that the disciples (whom I believe represented the Church in the passage under discussion) asked the question. From this writer's perspective, there are two reasons most conclude the Church is not in view in this passage. The first is to add further support for a pre-Tribulation Rapture and second to dismiss the Scriptural evidence that God does not remove His people from suffering (cf. Philippians 1:29) and persecution.

I have already discussed the relationship between the gospel of Matthews and the Church. So I see no further need to rehash it here except to reemphasize when prophecies involving the end-time are examined, it would be difficult not to conclude that much of it applies to the Church. Also, the term *falling away* by its nature has someone in mind that was once a part of that which they have now deserted. The Jews, even in a superficial sense, have never claimed to be part of those who have accepted Jesus of Nazareth not only as the Messiah but the Son of God, Savior of the world, and King of kings. I might add, one of the main reasons they wanted to stone Him was because He made such claims. I dare say that, if Jesus made this same claim to the Jews today, they would still call Him a blasphemer and liar. This is perhaps the most difficult hurdle to overcome in making this statement apply to Jews only.

Before continuing, I need to digress for a moment to take a closer look at the term *falling away*, because it is critical to our understanding of this first event of which Paul speaks. Not only did Paul use this term but our Lord used it in His characterization of this mass exodus from the Church in the last days. The term itself comes from the Greek word *apostasia* (a-pos-tas-ee-ah), which transliterates, or crosses directly over into our English word *apostasy.* Although it can carry the idea of someone who has knowledge of God, such knowledge is superficial and therefore not rooted. At best, it is a belief based solely upon intellect and not one of trusting in Christ as Lord and Savior. On the other hand, those who know God in an intimate way will never leave Him, no matter how hard-pressed. They will hold on and will become stronger during these times, not necessarily because of their own strength, but the strength and power of the Holy Spirit. It is God's power that began our salvation and He will keep on working in us until we are glorified and perfected (Romans 8:29–30; Philippians 1:6).

Furthermore, Christians are baptized into the Body of Christ and have become partakers of His divine nature (cf. 1 Corinthians 12:12–13; 2 Peter 1:4). Paul adds clarity to Peter's statement by stressing that we are "members of His body, of His flesh and of His bones" (Ephesians 5:30 KJV). Based on these two passages, we can conclude that Christians falling away from the Church is similar to an arm or leg falling off from a human body as a natural process. Both believer and nonbeliever alike would laugh and scoff (and rightly so) at such an absurd statement since its irrationality is clear to all. If such a notion is unthinkable, ridiculous, and impossible for our physical body, why would we think any less of the union with our Lord being so easily broken?

Salvation must never be thought of in terms of our power, but God's. The faith needed to keep one in times of trouble is much more than the type that can be mustered up by our own human strength. It is supernatural and has been nurtured and molded through the fires of tribulations, trials, and personal experiences. The New Testament Letter of James bring this point home in the first chapter of his letter where he states the purpose of trials are not only to grow our faith, but give us patience (cf. Romans 5:3–4). This is the reason Christians should welcome trials. They are the means by which God has chosen to increase our faith and glorify Him. In his letter to the Church at Philippi, Paul tells them (and us through them) that God has not only granted us the gift of faith (belief), but also the gift of suffering as well (Philippians 1:29). In that passage, the Greek word for *gift* is sometimes translated as *grace* elsewhere in the New Testament. Based on this and the third verse of the first chapter of the epistle of James, it seems the gift of suffering is an essential element of salvation. Left to our own we would never do much to grow spiritually, therefore God gives us the gift of suffering. It is during these times that we call on Him. As He brings us through these situations, we learn to depend on Him more and more, thereby increasing our trust and faith in Him. From the writer's perspective, the reason that a large majority of the Church in America looks at this idea as being strange and "ungodlike" is due largely to the false teachings of the prosperity and faith movement. In reality, any such teaching, according to Scripture, dishonors God and inhibits spiritual growth (Philippians 1:29).

Finally, as stated before, we mustn't forget the Holy Spirit is the One who began our salvation. He will not stop halfway and cast us aside. We can be assured that He will finish what He has begun (Philippians 1:6). Although this is not a chapter on eternal security, I do feel it needs to be mentioned briefly because of its connection to this idea that a believer can fall away from the Church. Our greatest assurance that we will never abandon Christ is based on His own Word, His power and promises that He holds us securely in His loving hands (cf. John 10:29).

The point of all this is to state, as I understand it, what the Scripture teach about the impossibility of Christians apostatizing. Our ultimate salvation does not depend on our holding on to God's hands, nor does it depend on our striving with all our strength, hoping but never being sure whether we will make it to heaven or not. Teachers that teach such dangerous errors should be utterly ashamed, since Scripture offers no support for such views. For a believer to somehow be saved and then suddenly decide to fall from the grace of God would mean that he or she has the ability to overcome God's sovereign will and power. The mere thought of this is not only absurd, but is the height of arrogance (cf. John 3:16; 6:39–40, 43–44, 47, 51, 54; Ephesians 1:3–9).

As the Good Shepherd, our Lord stressed this same truth in the tenth chapter of John's gospel when He said, "My Father, who has given them to me, is greater than all, no one can snatch them out of my Father's hand" (John 10:29 KJV). Based on these truths, we can be certain that when Jesus and Paul spoke of those who would fall away from the Church, they could not have had in mind those who have been born of the Spirit of God.

Having concluded that those who will comprise the great falling away cannot be Christians, let us try to look into the reasoning that would cause such a mass exodus from an institution that has been so foundational for many throughout the centuries.

Since its conception, the Church has been a place of comfort and a place of help for those in need, both spiritually and physically. To understand why many will no longer seek the Church as a place of solace, we need only read about the persecution inflicted upon the early Church. We can also look at the persecution of modern-day Christians in China, Sudan, Pakistan, Iran, and many other countries where religious freedom is only a dream. These churches show the undeniable fact that the Church is always strongest during her hour of testing, trials, and persecution. In other words, a light always shines brightest when placed in the darkest room.

As stated earlier, this idea of the Church undergoing persecution is foreign to most Christians in the West. The main reason for this is that some have forgotten, and others have never been exposed to this side of Christianity. When seen from God's perspective, suffering is as natural for Christians as breathing. This is why Paul tells us that "we must through much tribulation enter the kingdom of God" (Acts 14:22 KJV).

In anticipation of the obvious question of why we have been spared from persecution in America and other western countries, I can only accredit it to God's love, mercy, grace, and providence. While we enjoy this blessing in its season, we must and should prepare ourselves for the time when we too will have to suffer for the sake of our Lord. Such preparation involves supporting those in the household of faith who are undergoing suffering prayerfully and financially. At the same time, we are to be storing God's Word in our hearts. Realizing the time is coming and, in fact, may be closer than any of us would like to think, when our faith too will be tried and tested.

Before His departure, our Lord Himself warned that persecution would eventually come to all those who love Him. This was stated not as a possibility but a certainty. There should not be any confusion or doubt about what the Lord said or meant when He made this statement. The personal trials and abuses that we receive from family, friends, neighbors, and coworkers are no doubt trying on us, but such acts were not the only ones He had in mind. The intensity of the trials and tribulation referred to in His statement is borne out by the word He uses for tribulation. It comes from the Greek word *thlipsis* (thlip-sis) and means "to be placed or squeezed under extreme pressure." It accurately describes the terror and evil endured by the early Christians who according to the writer of the New Testament epistle of Hebrew "were stoned," and some "were sawn asunder" for their faith. Lest anyone believes these were just the exaggerations or imaginations of biblical writers, they need only examine the writings of secular historians who have left us vivid accounts of those early days of Christianity. Their pages recorded the horror and terror suffered by those who were used as human torches, fed to lions, boiled alive, tarred, and many other atrocities to inhumane and numerous to mention. However, through it all, they not only endured them willingly but did so with joy, realizing they were taking part in the suffering of their Lord.

Here lies the heart and soul of why I believe persecution will serve as the key cause in driving away those who were never part of the true Church. It will boil down to a matter of loyalty to Christ or love of life. When faced with these choices, those who were only part of the physical church will waste little or no time deserting the spiritual Church and all that she stands for, especially as the world turns against her. They will not find anything redeeming about rejoicing or suffering to the point of death for Jesus, who at best was only a good man in their sight. Lacking the Holy Spirit and saving faith, they will be unwilling and unable to stand and endure suffering for Jesus Christ.

CHAPTER 4

CHRISTIANS AMID PERSECUTION

There shall come a great falling away.
—2 Thessalonians 2:3

As we continue our discussion on the great falling away, the idea of the "hard sayings" of God comes to mind. Why would God allow His children to go through such pain and agony? Before we take on the answer to that question, perhaps it would be good to first ask some pointed questions of ourselves. First, are we any better than those who have gone before us? Despite their small number, they turned the world upside down. In contrast, not only are we greater in number, we have the added advantage of mass transportation and communication through the medium of satellite, cable television, shortwave radio, and the granddaddy of them all—the internet. With all these various means of communication available to us, there is almost no place in the world where the gospel cannot be heard, and usually, heard live and simultaneously. Yet, even with our religious freedom and advances in technology, our impact on the world is relatively small when compared to the early Church. What price have we paid for our Lord? What crosses have we borne? Too many Christians believe the one or two hours put in on Sunday morning is more than enough sacrifice for our Lord, and even that time most Christians do begrudgingly and irreverently.

Consider this fact: out of the seven churches mentioned in Revelation, Smyrna was the only one commended for her faithfulness while under persecution. The name *Smyrna* itself speaks of persecution, of suffering and death. Amid slanderers, idolaters, and all manner of evil works pressing on her from every side, the small church in Smyrna remained faithful to Christ. As a result of their faithfulness they became ostracized and cut off from the world because of their peculiar character and conduct. Some lost their lives, jobs, businesses, and no doubt became homeless and destitute, yet they did not lose hope and faith in their Lord.

Even though they were already suffering tremendously, Christ did not tell them to expect relief; instead they were to prepare themselves for more (Revelation 2:10). In other words, with the commendation of verses eight and nine of the second chapter of Revelation came the declaration that their persecution would continue for ten days (Revelation 2:8–11). Whether these were literal days or symbolic of a much longer period should not be the focus. The primary message of the passage is that the Lord does not automatically remove His people from trials and tribulations, even though our loved ones and friends may be dying all around us. Perhaps one reason that Jesus told His disciples that He would be with them always is because He knew that "in this world, you will have persecution." He wanted them, as well as us, to know that despite what the world may throw at us, we need not fear or dread because He will always be with us.

Admittedly passages such as Revelation 3:10 would seem to somehow contradict this truth, but when this verse is read and read contextually, no such conclusion can be drawn. For example, the word Jesus used for *keep* in that verse is the Greek word *Tereo* (tay-reh-o). Dr. Zodhiates, in his Word Study Dictionary defines this word as, "a warden, guard. To keep an eye on, watch, and therefore to guard, keep." On the particular verse in question, he further defines this word as "keeping for the fulfillment of the prophecy" (Spiros Zodhiates, *The Complete Word Study Dictionary New Testament*, AMG Publishers, 1992).

Based on these definitions, it would seem that Christ did not have in mind removal of the Church when He made this statement, but instead divine protection. The use of this same word in our Lord's High Priestly Prayer recorded in the seventeenth chapter of the gospel of John supports this conclusion. In verse fifteen of that chapter, He prays to His Father that He "shouldest keep them from the evil one." Removal from the evil one is obviously not His petition or desire. Contextually, it does not fit since the point of the prayer is

- to confirm the successful completion of the task given Him;
- to confirm He had glorified the Father while on earth;
- His request that His Father now glorify Him with the glory He had with Him before the foundation of the world;
- His revelation of the Father to the disciples;
- His protection of all those given to Him by the Father;
- His request to the Father to protect and keep them in unity;
- His sanctification of the disciples and His sending them into the world;
- the unity of all Christians with Christ and God, so the world will know that the Father sent him;
- that Christians will see the glory of Christ; and
- His continuous lasting love and revelation within all Christians.

By looking at the other six churches and the words used to describe them, we can better understand this statement in Revelation 3:10. For example, look at the language used in His message to the church at Ephesus. They're told that if they did not repent and start doing their first works He was going to "come unto thee quickly, and will remove thy candlestick" (Revelation 2:5). When He told the church of Ephesus that their candlestick would be removed, He meant just that—physical removal from their location. Now if He used *removed* there to suggest physical removal, why not use it again when addressing the Philadelphian church? The seven letters were not individual letters to each church but part of the one scroll containing the revelation given to John. Therefore, each congregation would have read, or at least had access, to all seven letters since copying was unavailable. Additionally, since those being addressed were living in the same geographical region, language would not have been a barrier. If Christ wanted to infer physical removal, He would not have used a different word, but one whose meaning would be clear and well-defined. To do otherwise would have caused the same kind of confusion seen in the Church today.

It would be difficult to find any suggestion of our Lord implying that it is His or the Father's will or desire to remove Christians out of the world during the tribulation period. The emphasis throughout His prayer is that His Father would keep the unity, love and protection of all Christians. Based on this, the only conclusion that can be drawn from the word *keep* is, if it means to guard or protect in the seventeenth chapter of John (vv. 12, 15), it must also carry the same meaning in Revelation 3:10.

There is a good illustration of this in the Old Testament. When God sent the plagues on Egypt, His people were clearly unaffected by them because of God's divine protection (cf. Exodus 8:22, 26; 9:4, 6; 10:23; 11:7; 12:13). God could have removed them from the land but He did not. I believe He will act in like manner during the time of the tribulation period. Since God has not chosen to reveal to us how He will keep us, we need not waste time trying to figure it out. What we do have is His faithfulness displayed through His servants of the Old and New Testament, as well as modern-day martyrs.

Because it is possible to take one or two passages and build an entire doctrine, we must exercise caution even here. Therefore, I direct the reader's attention to the seventeenth chapter of Revelation as further evidence that the Church will be severely persecuted in the last days. In verse six of that chapter, we find John looking at a vision of a woman described as "being drunk with the blood of the saints" (v. 6). Two things are obvious in this verse and the overall passage. First, John could not be speaking of a literal woman. This we can be dogmatic about because of the angel's interpretation in verse nine where John is told the woman sits on seven mountains. This single fact proves that she is symbolic, for what woman is there that can sit on seven mountains. Not only does she sit on seven mountains, but according to verse nineteen, she is also a city. Whether this city is Rome or some other city is not the issue. John is clearly told that at some future date (this has to be future since the events given from chapter four onward are described as those things which shall be here after), Christians, identified as saints in the passage, will undergo intense persecution from a city surrounded by seven mountains.

Second, the woman was drunk, not with wine, but the blood of the saints. Again, we can be sure of its meaning because again in verse fourteen, John is told that these (referring to the beast and the ten kings) will wage war against the saints. This is the second time that such descriptive language has been used of Christians in the book of Revelation, the first being verse seven of Revelation thirteen. There, he makes a clear inference that the Beast will not only persecute Christians but will be given power to overcome some of them. This would add much clarity to how this woman, working in league with the ten kings, could become drunk with the blood of people. This undoubtedly has reference to the saints, who were more than likely killed for their refusal to worship the beast.

This might also explain the concern voiced by the saints already around God's throne in Heaven (Revelation 6:9–10). If there was ever a place in the Bible where God could have made it plain that Christians will escape the tribulation period, surely it would have been here, yet His response is that they were to "wait a little longer, until the number of their fellow servants and brothers who were to be killed as they were, should be fulfilled" (Revelation 6:11 KJV). Based on this statement, not only will the Church be here during the tribulation period, but there is a set number of Christians that will be martyred during this time. This particular issue will be revisited in much more detail in a later chapter.

Both passages confirm Christ's own words, "Then shall be great tribulation, such as was not since the beginning of the world to this time, no, nor ever shall be" (Matthew 24:21). As stated before, when the word *tribulation* is used in scripture, it normally carries with it the idea of intense suffering, most of the time to the point of death. It's difficult now to imagine that a time will come when Christianity will become a crime of the state punishable by death because of our country's constitution. However, we need only think back to the Church's early beginning, not just the persecution by the Caesars, but the Church of Rome. Thousands of Christians were killed or persecuted by her while all along believing she was doing God's will. According to Revelation seventeen, history will apparently repeat itself, except this time on a much larger scale.

Therefore, I believe the Bible speaks of an event called the great falling away and will be the most visible sign the Second Coming is near. This great apostasy will not be a desertion by Christians (though some may leave the institution because of doubt), but those unbelievers identified by Christ as tares.

CHAPTER 5

AFTER THE APOSTASY

And that man of sin be revealed, the son of perdition.
—2 Thessalonians 2:3

On the heels of the great falling away will come the antichrist, a man who will epitomize evil. Simply put, he will stand against and oppose all that is Christ, and therefore, all that is God. The prefix *anti* is used of someone who opposes a specific person, social issue, or idea. However, when used of the antichrist, there is a dual meaning in view. He will be the ultimate enemy of Christ and will also try (and to a certain extent, succeed) to pass himself off as Christ, the Anointed of Israel. Through his craftiness and initial bias toward the Jews, he will be able to deceive them into believing that he is their long-awaited Messiah and king. To the world, he will present himself as being the only one that has the solutions to all its turmoil, woes, conflicts, and economical calamities. As a result, every single leader, seemingly with the approval of their citizenry, will willingly turn over their sovereignty and freedom to him. He will be—in the truest sense of the word—a world ruler! The church will be the lone beacon of truth in regard to his real identity and purpose. This being the case, she will become the prime target of his wrath and hatred.

However, according to most preachers and teachers, this is of little or no relevance to the church, since she will not be here when the antichrist appears on the world's stage. My only question to such a notion is "What would be the point in Paul's mentioning him at all, if the very people he was addressing would not even be here?" If the church is raptured by this time, who is it that Paul was warning or teaching? What significance would it be to the Thessalonians (or to us) to be warned of an event that would not involve us? If his (Antichrist) appearance must occur after the Rapture, it seems to this writer that Paul's mentioning of him was not only pointless, but deceiving as well. After all, his whole point in writing this second letter to the Thessalonians was to calm their fears and put them back on the right track about the Second Coming and The Day of the Lord. His primary means of doing this was to revisit his teaching on this period of time and to focus on the fact that specific events would take place before it happened.

To better understand the Thessalonians' concern, we should perhaps take a brief look at the term *Day of the Lord*. I believe this term is unique to the last days and refers to the period from the tribulation to the final Judgment after the millennium reign of Christ. Although the term itself is more prevalent in the Old Testament, its teaching is very much part of the New Testament. For example, early in the book of Matthew, John the Baptist points out that Jesus would "baptize you with the Holy Ghost and with fire" (Matthew 3:11 NKJV). The term *fire* in that passage refer to the Lord's final Judgment of the world by fire. Or notice again in the Olivet Discourse recorded in both Matthew (chapter 24) and Luke's gospel (chapter 21:25–37) where we're given a detail breakdown of the events that will comprise this time. Peter's second epistle, Paul's epistles to the Corinthians, Thessalonians, and Jude are all books that speak directly to this issue in the New Testament.

About this day, the Old Testament prophet, Amos, prophesied to Judah that, "it is a day of darkness not light." That prophecy sums up what the world can expect when that "day" is upon us: a time of darkness and not light. The Thessalonians' confusion centered around this time period. Paul stressed that the great falling away and appearance of the man of sin must take place before this time comes.

Who is this person, and how will the world recognize him? Perhaps no other book in the Bible gives a more detail picture of his origin, character, exploits and ambitions than does the book of Daniel. In the seventh chapter of that book, he is the little horn. In the ninth chapter, he is the prince of the people who would eventually destroy the city of Jerusalem (v. 27). These two chapters as well as chapters eight and ten provide critical information about the antichrist. But it is the latter portions of chapter eleven (vv. 36–45) that gives a detailed breakdown about his rule and character.

In these chapters, it becomes clear that God has revealed much about this man to us through the Prophet Daniel. However, at the time Daniel received the prophecy, it had little, if any, relevance to him, his people, or his time. Daniel's own questioning of the angel in chapter twelve and the angel's response to him that he was to "go thy way, Daniel: for the words are closed up and sealed till the time of the end" bear this out (Daniel 12:9 KJV). The words of the prophecy were neither for him nor his immediate generation; they would remain a mystery and sealed until the end-times. It is for our time that God gave those prophecies to Daniel. I believe that this is one of the main reasons for the sudden interest in eschatology today. It is a sign of God's Spirit illuminating and stirring the hearts and minds of His people. He is giving us understanding and wisdom about the events that will lead up to His Son's Second Coming and the events that will characterize it.

This also explains why passages such as Matthew twenty-four, the epistles to the Thessalonians, and Revelation, and other Old Testament books give us such a detail picture of the future. This is especially true as it relates to the man of sin and our ability to be able to recognize him. It should not come as a surprise that God would reveal these things to us. After all, His desire is that we be ready for this time in history so we will not lose heart. It is in answer to God's own rhetorical question posed in Genesis eighteen: "Shall I hide from Abraham that thing which I do" (Genesis 18:17). Just as He would not hide from Abraham the future destruction of Sodom and Gomorrah, neither will He hide from Abraham's spiritual descendants that which He is about to do to this evil and perverse generation. These are the reasons that we need to read and study the end-times.

CHAPTER 6

GOD'S REVELATION OF THE END

And four great beasts came up from the
sea, diverse one from another.

—Daniel 7:3

I believe the Old Testament book of Daniel is perhaps one of the most important books in the Bible when it comes to teaching and understanding biblical prophecy. This does not mean Daniel is the only book we should consider in the Old Testament since others such as Isaiah, Joel, Amos, and Zechariah provide valuable information about the events that will characterize the latter days. They, along with Daniel and Revelation, are integral parts of the whole subject of eschatology.

The book of Daniel provides specific details about how we will be able to recognize the Antichrist when he appears. Reading Daniel is almost like reading a summary of world history from the Babylonian Empire to the last judgment. His specificity about the rise and fall of the four major world empires continues to baffle historians and skeptics alike. The accuracy of the origins of these empires, their rulers, downfall, and duration is of such that many infer that, more than likely the book of Daniel was written after these events took place by an unknown author and later accredited to Daniel.[1]

---

[1] MacArthur, John, *The Future of Israel* Audio Series.

It is easy to understand how one could arrive at such a conclusion. It was a common practice in that day for an obscure author to gain credibility for his writings by assigning a well-known figure's name, such as a prophet's, to his own work. This accounts for much, if not all, the writings of the Apocrypha. We reject this assumption outright because we believe in the inerrant, infallible, and inspired Word of God. The accuracy of the Bible is the result of Divine Inspiration and not human authors.

This is especially true when it comes to prophecy. The popularity of horoscopes, psychic readings, and other predictors of the future have found a new popularity within our culture. The main reason being man's insatiable need to know the future, even though he hasn't the power to neither add nor take away from what God has already determined. Who knows how much money people spend annually on the psychic networks, tarot cards, and palm readers and such as a means of plotting their daily life? However, the inaccuracies of these modern-day psychics and readers were not true of Daniel. His gift of understanding all visions and dreams was "ten times better than all the magicians and astrologers that were in all his (Nebuchadnezzar) realm" (Daniel 1:17b, 20 KJV). This is the reason he was able to intercede for the Chaldeans (and himself) through Arioch, after King Nebuchadnezzar's sentenced them to death after being unable to interpret his dream (Daniel 2:14–16).

Daniel's intimacy with God was the reason for his boldness. That relationship assured Daniel he would be able to interpret the dream, not by his ability, but the supernatural power of God. Seen in Nebuchadnezzar's dream is the fact that God does at times work through pagans and unbelievers to reveal His will. Such was the case with Nebuchadnezzar (cf. Ezra 1:1–2), a pagan who knew nothing about Daniel's God. However, despite this flaw, God not only used him in revealing to us events of the last days but also brought the king to the realization that He was the "God of gods."

The details revealed in Nebuchadnezzar's dream about his kingdom and those that would succeed him were so accurate that it is not surprising that he recognized Daniel's God as the true God. As a matter of fact, an accurate and verifiable summary of history is set before us when Nebuchadnezzar's dream and Daniel's vision recorded in the seventh chapter of Daniel are interpreted together. If there were no secular historical references available at all, these two chapters would be enough to understand the origin, fall and succession of all the world empires from Babylon to the end of time (Dr. John MacArthur, *The Kingdoms of the World*).

According to Scripture, King Nebuchadnezzar's dream troubled him to the point where he lost his sleep. In today's vernacular, we would say that he had a nightmare so terrifying and so real that he woke up in a cold sweat. The dream deeply troubled and disturbed him. The fact that he was unable to go back to sleep was not the main reason he was troubled. His problem was with the content of the dream on the one hand and his inability to remember it on the other.

The responsibility of the wise men and astrologers of the Babylonian kingdom was to interpret dreams. Therefore, the King immediately sent for them so they could tell him the meaning of his dream. However, this would not be a simple task because the king had added a twist. Not only were they to tell him the interpretation of the dream, but its content as well. After hearing this unusual request, one can only imagine the bewilderment and concern that must have come over them. While it was true that they probably did have some limited ability to foretell the future, such predictions and interpretations were no more accurate than the self-proclaimed prophets and psychics mentioned earlier.

In reading this passage of Scripture, I do not think the immediate concern was their inability to interpret the king's dream as much as it was for the qualifier added to the king's command. It is interesting that when they could not do as the king had asked, his first response was not one of giving them the benefit of the doubt or that maybe the question was unreasonable. Instead, it was one of suspicion and anger. At this point, he did not want excuses. If they could not tell him his dream, maybe it was because they never had this ability in the first place and had been deceiving him all along. While he might have gone along with them in the past, it would not be so now. This matter was one of utmost urgency, and if these men did not provide him an answer immediately, they would suffer the fate of their failure—death! Obvious the king believed this question to be fair and reasonable. That is, if they were who they claimed to be, this should not have been a problem.

His conclusion was not far-off and supports the New Testament teaching that only those indwelt by the Spirit can know the things of God. If God does not condescend and communicate to us in a manner we can understand, we will never know His will and purposes. This is the reasoning God gave Daniel a vision of the king's dream after he had prayed, not only for understanding, but to reveal to him its content as well.

As we examine the dream, there are some key elements about it that helps us understand its importance. The first thing seen is Daniel's acknowledgment that it is the God in heaven that reveals secrets and will therefore make known to him the king's dream. With this statement, he clearly affirms that God is the only one who knows the heart and mind of man. He chooses how and through whom He will reveal His will—if He chooses to do so at all. In recognizing God's power in this area, Daniel glorifies Him and at the same time, draws a clear distinction between Him and the pagan gods worshipped by the king and his "wise men." He further lets the king know that his ability to reveal and interpret the dream is not because he is any wiser or more learned than anyone else. It is that his God has graced him to be able to interpret the dream.

Daniel's confession is important for our day. All too often many see God as a "Heavenly Bellhop" obliged to always respond positively to their prayers. This thinking did not characterize Daniel's or any prophet when they petitioned God. They fully recognized God as being the Sovereign One who moves as He wills in the lives of both the Christian and the unsaved. He fully expected and believed that God would hear his petition and answer it, not out of duty, but because of his grace and mercy. That's why he responded to the king as he did. He wanted him to know that God, and God alone is worthy of all thanks, all praise, all adoration, and honor. He was only a willing vessel that God has graciously chosen to speak through. After all, if God used a donkey to speak His word, who among men can boast (Numbers 22:28)?

It is for their sakes God revealed the dream. It is unclear about whom Daniel has in mind by the term *their* in this verse (Daniel 2:30), and since it is not in the original manuscript, we need not linger on it here. What is and should be our focus is God wanted the king to know the intent of his dream.

What a beautiful picture of God's love, mercy, and compassion on Nebuchadnezzar, who just a few short years earlier had pillaged the city of Judah, burned the house of the Lord (2 Kings 7–8), and plucked out the eyes of His servant King Zedekiah. Yet God poured His grace on him, despite all he had done against His people.

No one should judge Nebuchadnezzar too harshly since he acted out of ignorance. Who among us can rightly say that we deserve God's grace and mercy any more than he? Are we more deserving of His love? Did He not send His only begotten Son to take the punishment on Calvary's cross for sinners worse than he? I believe John Newton said it best: it is only God's "amazing grace" that has saved us.

Second, Daniel told the king the dream concerns things of the latter days. This is the point where many go wrong as they choose to ignore Scripture and go their own way by either spiritualizing this whole dream or making the starting point of the prophecy Egypt or some other empire. There is little or no disagreement on the fact the term *latter-days* is a reference to the last days. Where disagreement does comes in, is identifying the head of the first beast in chapter seven is Babylon, or some other empire.

A misinterpretation of this part of the dream will lead to a wrong understanding of the whole prophecy. Therefore to help us, and no doubt to prevent confusion, God provides the point of reference in the latter portion of the thirty-eighth verse of chapter two by identifying Nebuchadnezzar as being the "head of gold." As stated earlier, the purpose of the dream was to reveal the kingdoms or empires that would have sovereign rule over most of the then known civilized world during the time of their reign.

The book of Daniel consists of two sections. The first one consists of chapters one through six and involve God communicating to pagan kings with Daniel being the interpreter. The second section, consisting of chapters seven through twelve, is God communicating to Daniel through visions with angels being the interpreters. Therefore, when it came time for God to reveal to Nebuchadnezzar what would happen to his kingdom once he died (cf. Daniel. 2:29), he gave him the dream recorded in Daniel chapter two. God has not chosen to reveal to us why He gave Nebuchadnezzar and Daniel the same prophecy. One possible reason pointed out by Dr. John MacArthur is that Daniel's vision is God speaking to His servant. Therefore, it is man and his kingdoms from God's perspective. On the other hand, the dream given to Nebuchadnezzar is man's own view of himself, his self-reliance and perceived ability to control his own destiny.[1] To Nebuchadnezzar, his kingdom was one of splendor, of magnificence, and power brought to that point by his own making. The idea of a Sovereign Lord fixing and controlling the boundaries of his and all other kingdoms before time began (Acts 17:26; cf. Romans 13:1) was unimaginable to him.

Since the Fall, man in general has always regarded himself, his achievements and successes in this way. Pride was man's problem in King Nebuchadnezzar's time and it remains so today. Pride is the one sin where man's sinful nature shows itself and shows itself clearly, because it says of God, "I don't need you." In a sense, pride is man placing himself in a position of exaltation, something he has neither earned nor deserve.

However, the seventh chapter of Daniel shows man as he is. When God looks at man says the Psalmist, He declares there is none righteous, none good and none seeking after Him (cf. Psalm 14:1–3). When Adam sinned, he lost the beauty and glory that characterized man at creation. This is not to say that man in his fallen state cannot produce works of beauty, or perform generous acts toward his fellowman, since many do so every day. However, such acts come from a heart that is sinful and self-centered, seeking to gratify self and not to glorify God. This is the reason that when God reveals the nations of the world to Daniel, He portrays them as beasts, ferocious, grotesque, and hostile. So in King Nebuchadnezzar's eyes, his kingdom

---

[1] Dr. John MacArthur, "Daniel 7, Part 2", *The Coming Kingdom*, Audio Series.

was majestic, beautiful, and unparalleled in power; to God it was ugly, vile, and lacking of anything virtuous (Dr. John MacArthur, *The Kingdoms of the World*). Seen in the chart below are the similarities between these two chapters.

Nebuchadnezzar's Dream (Daniel 2)	Daniel's Dream (Daniel 7)
Head of Gold	Beast like a Lion with Eagle's Wings
Chest and Arms of Silver	Beast Like a Bear
Belly and Thighs of Bronze	Beast Like a Leopard with four wings
Legs of Iron	Dreadful and Terrible Beast with Iron Teeth
Feet of Iron and Clay	Ten Horns
Stone not cut out with hand	The Everlasting Kingdom

What we have in Daniel's vision is clarification that the first world power symbolized by the head of the statue in Nebuchadnezzar's dream is Babylon. It seems as if though God has gone out of His way to provide plain evidence to this effect. Not only does He say it outright in chapter two, He reveals it to us again in His description of the first beast's wings being plucked and "lifted up from the earth and made to stand upon the feet as a man" in the seventh chapter of Daniel (v. 4).

In saying this, He was clearly alluding to the horrible dream recorded in the fourth chapter of Daniel. Unlike the three succeeding kingdoms, Nebuchadnezzar was almost, if not synonymous with the kingdom of Babylon itself. He was a true monarch. He exercised total rule over his kingdom and subjects. When he decreed an edict, it was irrevocable. In his eyes, there was no one greater than he, no other power and no other kingdom greater than his. Such arrogance and pride on his behalf was the reason that God gave him another dream in chapter four. In it, he and his kingdom was again the focus. This time, he did not bother calling for the wise men but sent for Daniel immediately for the dream's interpretation. The dream was God's way of telling King Nebuchadnezzar he was going to drive him from his natural habitat into the field. There he would eat grass like an ox, his hair would become like the feathers of an eagle's, and his nails like bird claws (Daniel 4:25, 33). The main purpose of this was to destroy his pride and remind him that all that he had was not his doing. God wanted to show him in a real and personal way that "the most High ruleth in the kingdom of men, and giveth it to whomever he will, and setteth up over it the basest of men" (Daniel 4:17 KJV). This is the meaning of the wings being plucked from the lion in Daniel's dream recorded in chapter seven, the indisputable symbol of king Nebuchadnezzar's downfall. Nebuchadnezzar soared as an eagle on the wind of his own pride until God plucked his wings. It was the only road that could have bought him to the reality that he was nothing without God; a fact he willingly recognized after God restored him from his bestial state (Daniel 4:34).

The next three kingdoms or empires that would follow Babylon again are implicitly, if not directly, identified for us in the seventh chapter of Daniel by the second, third, and fourth beast. The inter-pretation is as follows. The second beast is Medo-Persia, symbolized by the silver chest and arms of the statue. Daniel chapter five records this succession of power by the simple statement that "Darius the Median took the kingdom" (Daniel 5:31 KJV).

The third empire symbolized by the bronze stomach and thighs in Nebuchadnezzar's dream and the leopard with the four wings in Daniel's vision aptly portrays the Grecian Empire. Alexander the Great, who was, and perhaps still, regarded as the greatest military general of all time, led Greece to become one of the greatest empires there ever was. As the empires before him, he was able to subdue and rule most of the then-known civilized world. What was amazing about this was the fact he achieved this feat before he reached his mid-thirties.

When I think of Alexander the Great, I see the sovereign hand of God moving on a man in doing something that would eventually become the foundation for the proclamation of the gospel. Not by his conquests or magnificent scientific expeditions, but the spreading of the Greek culture, especially the language, throughout his empire. When Rome came on the scene, there was already a universal lan-guage known and spoken throughout the world—Greek. This one fact along with Rome's ability to build huge networks of roads that connected the entire kingdom would later serve as the means of writing and spreading the gospel throughout the world.

Daniel could give us a picture of the first three beasts, because they were similar to those familiar to him. However, it seems that he could not find words to describe the fourth beast. All he could say about it was that it was "dreadful and terrible, and strong exceedingly; and had great iron teeth." According to the latter description of this beast or whatever it was, it seemingly had the strength to destroy and devour everything and anything in its path. How often have I watched cars being smashed by a crushing machine, so much so until the end product bore little or no likeness to its original state? This is the picture I think Daniel is trying to describe. There is little or no need to guess or argue that this last empire, symbolized by this fourth beast and the two legs of Nebuchadnezzar's dream clearly represented the Roman Empire. The symbolism of the iron teeth is as accurate a portrayal of the Roman legions as one can get. It was their strength, power, and ruthlessness that crushed and brought every enemy of Rome to their knees, and done so at times in the most brutal and horrible fashion. As a result, the Caesars of Rome were able to declare peace throughout the empire.

These were the four empires of the world set forth in Nebuchadnezzar's dream and Daniel's vision, Babylon, Medo-Persia, Greece, and Rome. Their glory and power being nothing more now than a dark memory recorded on the pages of history. With the exception of Rome, Babylon and the empires of Persia and Greece have ceased to exist in their former state. In other words, they are no longer regarded as being significant (even Iraq, which is modern-day Babylon) when it comes to world domination. Only Rome has begun a rebirth to her former state, power, and influence. If looked at objectively, one would see perfect fulfillment of the ten toes in Nebuchadnezzar's dream and the ten horns of the fourth beast in Daniel's vision in the form of the European Union. A comparison between maps of modern-day Europe to that of the Holy Roman Empire at its peak clearly supports this conclusion. We will look at this rebirth more closely in the next chapter.

CHAPTER 7

THE LITTLE HORN

There came up among them another little horn.
—Daniel 7:8

Whenever theologians and preachers began to talk about the European Union being the rebirth of the old Roman Empire, the world scoffs and all but calls them crazy. This should not come as a surprise to Christians since the word of God clearly states that this will be man's attitude in the last days. However, what is alarming is this same attitude being displayed among some within the church.

The first chapter of this book stressed the importance of Christians being watchful and observant of the signs unfolding before us. Those who fail to watch will not be left behind, but unprepared for the next great event on God's calendar—the formulation of the new Roman Empire—whose foundation is already solidly in place. Laws governing every aspect of Europeans' lives are already implemented by the governing heads of the European Union (EU). Borders have been erased creating a United States of Europe to allow travel and commerce between countries without the need of passports. With the introduction of the Euro in 1999, the EU became a major player on the world stage; both economically, socially and politically. Highlighting this reality was an article that appeared in the May–June 2001 Lamplighter magazine which stated that,

> according to the Rev. Dr. Ian Paisley, a Northern Ireland Protestant minister and member of the European Parliament, the woman on a beast is now the official picture of the EU. He points out the multimillion-dollar new parliament building in Brussels, Belgium, contains a dome with a colossal painting, three times life-size, of a woman riding a beast. In Strasbourg, France, the rival parliamentary building (the one with the Tower of Babel) features a mural of a naked woman riding a beast. Likewise, the new Brussels headquarters of the Council of Europe contains a bronze statue of a woman riding a beast, and the beast is depicted riding on waves, just as in Revelation 17. Scripture is being fulfilled before our eyes, for those with eyes to see.[1]

But can these statements justify such a bold, or in some people's minds, absurd statement about something that seems to be only possible in the movies or comic books? The answer to that question lies not in the fact that it was written or said by man, but the Word of God has already declared it! Its accuracy and power is dependent on God Himself who knows the end from the beginning. If nothing else, fulfillment of the dream and vision of Daniel and Nebuchadnezzar proves this. Who among historians and scholars can dispute the Bible's accuracy about the rise and fall of the most powerful empires the world has ever known? There are those who supposedly can use statistics and other measuring data to try to project where this or that country will be in so many years. But how has the accuracy of their prediction fared in comparison to God's?

---

[1] Alan Franklin, "The Religious Symbols of the European Union" The Lamplighter Magazine, May – June 2001, 10.

Having said that, let's look at the specific prophecy that talks about the rebirth of Rome. Notice the ten toes of the statue in Nebuchadnezzar's dream that match the ten horns on the beast in Daniel's vision. By looking at both chapters, we see two important traits that will characterize this new empire. The first one is its composition, described in Daniel chapter two as being a mixture of iron and clay. It does not take much to understand and realize that it would take a miracle to make these two unlikely elements bond naturally or any other way. By putting such a makeup before us, I believe God is letting us know that although there will be unity among this new confederation (or whatever its final state is), it will not be a strong one. Therefore, if it is to become the world power that it must, an exemplary leader must emerge. One who has the personality and leadership qualities that will be able to convince either by force or coercion, all parties to set aside their differences and not only come together as one, but appoint him as their leader. The personality symbolized as the little horn in Daniel's vision of the world empires will be such a leader. Many leaders within the European Union are already floating this idea stating that "committees do not work and they need more inspired leadership. German Foreign Minister Joschka Fischer repeated his call for a European government in July 2000, and said the European single currency—the Euro—was 'the first step to a federation.'" He added that he wanted a "powerful president."[1]

This writer believes that sometimes the world looks at its greatest leaders and secretly wishes that if only they all could be combined into one man. That wish will finally come to fruition in the man called Antichrist. It was during the Persian Gulf War the phrase "One World Order" came into prominence. Although many laughed at this idea or concept of a centralized government ruling the entire world, the Bible makes it clear that one day this will become a reality. As the Caesars ruled the world from Rome during the Old Roman Empire, so will one man rule the world from the seat of the revived Roman Empire!

---

[1] "German Foreign Minister floats idea of elected EU president," *The Financial Times*, July 7, 2000.

We first find him in the seventh chapter of Daniel (v. 8) in the person of the little horn. The term *little* is used in contradistinction with the other ten horns on the back of the fourth beast. In other words, as the little horn, he will be someone of little or no notoriety at first. However, despite this flaw, he will be able to rise from obscurity to power by plucking up three of the original ten horns. From the language used, it suggests that this leader overtakes three kings by force, or by some type of uprising or other violent action. Actions are in view in this verse. Daniel uses this same word of plucking the wings from the first beast in the fourth verse of chapter seven.

As a young boy on the farm, one of the things that I did not look forward to was plucking chicken feathers. Though the chicken was dead and unaware of what was happening, I could still imagine the pain that they would have felt if they were still alive. This was the imagery in mind when the writer used this word in verse four of Daniel chapter seven; one of tearing, of pulling the wings forcibly from the beast.

However, this is not the same use of the word *pluck* in verse eight of the seventh chapter of Daniel. There, it means to dig down or root up. In other words, it appears this man somehow removes these kings through cunning, subtlety and deception. The language suggests he will carry out this feat even before the three kings in question fully realize what's going on. To do this, he will have to be a master of deception, and the consummate strategist. His skill in diplomacy and oratory will be unparalleled in history.

During the sixties, I recall the various speeches made by the late Dr. Martin Luther King Jr. His oratorical abilities were astounding. When he spoke, one could not help but listen, even those who hated and despised him admired his ability to move and motivate those who heard him. The voice, the pitch, his stature; everything about him seemed so perfect. He was not alone in this area. There were others such as Churchill, John Kennedy, Ronald Reagan, Bill Clinton who also had this ability. However, all these men will be as children compared to this little horn's oratorical skills. Not only will he be a master orator, but he will also have the power to carry out whatever he speaks. Here lies true power; it is one thing to be able to speak well, but quite a different matter to be able to carry out to the letter what one speaks.

His superior intelligence will be another means of his success. verse eight of Daniel chapter seven confirms this in the words that he had "eyes like the eyes of man, and a mouth speaking great things." The emphasis on eyes in this verse is used not so much to describe his appearance, but instead to magnify his intelligence.

He will take great pride in his newfound power, so much so he will not only speak great things against others, but against God himself (Daniel 11:36). As Daniel continues his description of this man, we learn that his appearance was "more stout" than the other rulers. When placed against these others rulers, his appearance was more impressive and stately than all of them. Based on all that is said about this man, this writer believes he will not only speak like a great king and leader, but will even look and seemingly act the part. Like King Saul of Israel, his appearance will be that of a king (1 Samuel 9:2).

But what good is a king without an army? We spoke earlier of the achievements of the Roman legions, without which Ancient Rome could never have achieved the greatness and longevity that it enjoyed for over one thousand years. To ensure that order is upheld in his kingdom, and quickly squelch any uprising, the Antichrist will need a powerful military force. In achieving this feat, he will spare no expense in building such military might. If he is to worship anything or anyone, it will be the "god of fortresses," or literally "the god of force." However, even in such a controlled environment, there still will exist the need for incentives to keep the loyalty, dedication, and commitment of those serving him. To this end, he will reward those who recognize his rule with rulership and land (Daniel 11:38–39). They will become the instruments of his extended power and influence.

Added to this will be the fact that he will be an exceptional military strategist, leader, and negotiator. The fact he will be able to restore peace to the perpetual hot spot of the world—Israel (cf. Daniel 9:27)—demonstrates his military skill. We're not told how he's able to do this, but somehow, he will set up a covenant with Israel for seven years. The difficulty and obstacles being faced by those trying to accomplish the same feat today is another testimony to this man's diplomatic skills. Perhaps when faced with his military force, might and world dominion, the natural enemies in that region will willingly agree to peace.

So in this little horn, we have the man of all men. There will be no one equaled to him militarily, economically, politically, and socially. If he is to solve the myriads of problems that plague the world, such as hunger, economics, and wars between nations, he will have to be all this and more. As incredible and impossible as this may seem, he will perform these things in a manner that will absolutely astound the world. This man will so overwhelm the peoples of the world with all his feats, that every single person who is not saved will willingly give him their loyalty and worship. Those who rebel or reject his rule will pay with their life.

But how could such a task be possible? When one considers all the diversities that exist in the world, combined with the schisms and all the other idiosyncrasies that make the world what it is, how could one man bring unity to it? Daniel gives us a glance into how he will achieve this feat in the latter half of the eleventh chapter of his book. Notice first, that he will do as he wills. He will exalt himself above all gods, including those of his fathers, and in his arrogance and pride will speak "unheard-of things against the God of gods." He will blaspheme the name and character of God and will go one step further than Antiochus Epiphanes (who slaughtered a pig on the Temple's Altar) by sitting in the Holy of Holies and proclaim himself as God (Matthew 24:15; 2 Thessalonians 2:4).

When one looks at all he will do, Hitler, Mussolini, Nero, and all the other maniacs who wanted to be gods will seem like nothing when compared to this man. As if to further point out this person's total obsession of self and his passion for power, we're told that he will have no desire for women (Daniel 11:37). By this, I don't think the implication is that he will be a homosexual, but instead that women will have no appeal or interest to him, either sexually or emotionally. His only love is for himself, his kingdom, and the military might needed to keep it. Everything else will take a far backseat or no seat at all to these, his primary interest and concerns.

When one reads the interpretation given in the latter portion of chapter eleven about Antichrist, it becomes clear why Satan does not want this particular message known. It has always and remains his primary objective to interrupt, confuse, and destroy God's will for his people. He does this best when we ignore and do not study God's word.

CHAPTER 8

THE PRINCE THAT SHALL COME

And I saw a rider on the first horse.

—Revelation 6:2

It is not my intent to do a commentary on the book of Revelation (perhaps that will come later). However, it is the one book that is the consummation of all things and presents symbolically those things that are yet to happen in regard to the Lord's return. Therefore, since this is the blessed hope of all Christians, we must let Scripture speak to us about those things that must and will take place before the return of Christ. This is especially true as it relates to the Antichrist and the revived Roman Empire.

The events described in the first five chapters of Revelation are chronological. As a result, reading and interpreting the book up to that point is easy. However, once we reach chapter six, it becomes obvious the events depicted in the first two verses are not the only things that takes place at the opening of the first seal. The reasoning for this conclusion is the fact it opens with the Antichrist seemingly already declared as being ruler of the world. This is the only logical explanation for the white horse, empty bow, and the crown on his head.

The record of Creation in the first two chapters of the book of Genesis is a good example of what's being done in the first verses of the sixth chapter of Revelation. Chapter one of Genesis is a recollection of the creation, including Adam and Eve. However, what we have in that chapter is a summary of all God had done (Genesis 1:27–28). All the detail about how He made man from the dust of the earth, Adam's naming of the animals and Eve's being formed from his rib is given in the second chapter of Genesis (Genesis 2:7–25).

This is what I see happening in the sixth chapter of Revelation as it relates to the Antichrist. He comes on the scene, already crowned, victorious, and rides onto the world stage on the steed of conquerors and kings—the White Horse. But how was he able to perform this herculean task? Other portions of Revelation and Daniel provide information about how he was able to do this. Therefore, to get an understanding of chapter six, it is important to identify the chapters or events that led up to it.

The first thing is to establish the event that makes the identity of the Antichrist undeniable. Because of their accomplishments and prominence, many men were thought to be the Antichrist. To avoid making this same mistake Christians must be able to recognize him. The passage that provides us the information that will identify him beyond any reasonable doubt is the twenty-seventh verse of the ninth chapter of Daniel. According to this passage, two things will clearly identify Him:

- He will establish a covenant or a treaty of some sort between himself and Israel.
- The covenant will be for seven years.

If the leader in question does not meet these two requirements exactly, he cannot be the Antichrist. Once these two events take place, those with spiritual eyes will know the first seal of the sixth chapter of Revelation has opened. And, more importantly, God's timetable for the last seven years of the world has started. Therefore, Christians that are alive during this particular time can begin the final countdown to the end of the world. Do not confuse this with "date setting," since it is in line with God's own revelation given to us through the Seventy-Weeks of Daniel (discussed further in chapter 10) and not man's calculations or inferences.

To further help in the proper interpretation of how Antichrist comes to power, it is important to keep in mind one specific feature about how John wrote the book of Revelation, especially the visions. There are times when they summarize a very long period of time, such as the first few verses of chapter twelve. Sometimes they are of events that happen in heaven, while at other times they record what is happening on earth. Still there are times when we read of particular events that happened in the past combined with an event in the future. The latter portion of chapter twelve and all of chapter seventeen is an example of this kind of vision. Therefore, before we began our discussion, we need to first put the book of Revelation in some sort of logical order to understand the Antichrist's rise to power. The diagram (Illustration 1) below shows how I believe the book of Revelation is structured. Reading it in this fashion makes it easier to follow the natural progression of events that will usher in the Antichrist.

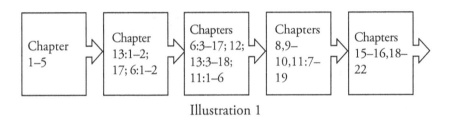

Illustration 1

In examining this chart, we find that in the order of events, chapter six comes after chapters thirteen (vv. 1–2) and seventeen (Illustration 2). The reasoning being, that both chapters (13 and 17) help us understand Antichrist's point of origin (chapter 13) and how he's able to rise to power so quickly (chapter 17).

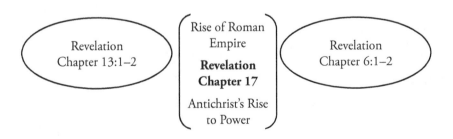

Illustration 2

Based on this, I believe the first two verses of chapter thirteen is the next logical sequence of events that helps us understand and interpret chapter six. If you notice, in those two verses, we see a beast coming up out of the sea. If taken by itself, the reader will undoubtedly arrive at the wrong interpretation. The reason for misinterpretations is because many fail to apply sound biblical hermeneutical principle to this passage. Therefore, they miss its logical connection to both chapters sixth and seventeen, and the seventh chapter of Daniel.

The first place to start from when interpreting these verses is to read them and find other verses that depict the same theme or message. In doing so, Scripture interprets Scripture and leads us to the correct conclusion. When this is done, we find there are two other passages in the Bible that become keys to unfolding the mystery surrounding the meaning of this beast in chapter thirteen.

But before going to them, we must examine the term *sea*. Sometimes the Bible uses this word symbolically as in Revelation 4:6 and 15:2. I do not believe this to be the case in the verses under consideration in chapter thirteen. This sea is literal, and its purpose is to point the reader to a specific geographical region of the world—in particular, the Mediterranean or Great Sea. The description of the beast's legs is the reason for saying this. They are not ones of any specific animal, but a combination of a lion, bear, and leopard. Here lies the reasoning for placing the seventh chapter of Daniel as part of Illustration 2. When these two verses are interpreted with Daniel, we have a clear picture of what's being said and why the sea is to be regarded as the Mediterranean.

We must keep in mind the seventh chapter of Daniel consists of a vision Daniel had where he saw four beasts: a lion, leopard, bear, and a fourth beast that was beyond description. A close look at the first verse of the thirteenth chapter of Revelation reveals that what we have in John's vision is a picture of Babylon (lion's leg), Persia (bear's leg), and Greece (leopard's leg). The only one seemingly missing is the fourth beast. A comparison of the description of the Beast in Revelation thirteen and the fourth beast of the seventh chapter of Daniel's vision reveals them to be one and the same. If this is the case, why is he not identified as the others, one might ask? The answer to that question lies in the fact that as the fourth beast in Daniel's dream was symbolic of the coming Roman Empire; the beast in the thirteenth chapter of Revelation is the Roman Empire revived. The ten horns support this conclusion. Therefore, the beast in the thirteenth chapter of Revelation is symbolic of both the old and future Roman Empire. The fact that his legs were of animals symbolizing Babylon, Persia, and Greece amplifies the power that this coming empire will have. It will be a combination of all that made ancient Babylon, Persia, Greece and Rome such a dominant force in their day. This also explains how the Antichrist will be able to come to world dominance so quickly. Like ancient Rome, he will have all this power behind him, making it impossible for any foe to challenge or defeat him.

But this leads to the question, "What about the seven heads?" The Holy Spirit identifies these heads in the seventeenth chapter of Revelation and adds further support that the sea mentioned in the thirteenth chapter of Revelation is the Mediterranean or at least that area of the world geographically. In chapter seventeen, an angel carries John (spiritually) into a wilderness where he sees a woman sitting on a scarlet-colored beast. A careful study of this chapter reveals the angel's description of seven rulers of Rome (v. 10). As we look at these kings, we see a line of kings or people the Antichrist comes from. By line, I do not mean genealogy, but line in the sense of specific emperors of Ancient Rome whose behavior, character, and rule the Antichrist will imitate, especially that of emperor worship. In other words, in verse ten, we read there are seven kings; five are fallen, or killed, and one is. The "one is" refers to the ruler currently on the throne during the writing of the book of Revelation. But a sixth is not yet come. That's because it refers to the ruler of the future empire of Rome—the Antichrist.

This is another point where many have gone wrong by interpreting this passage in Revelation as referring to a succession of world empires. Again, if we allow Scripture to interpret Scripture, we see this passage is an explanation of verse twenty-six of the ninth chapter of Daniel—in particular the phrase "and the people of the prince that shall come shall destroy the city and the sanctuary." We have already identified the phrase *the people* in that verse as being a reference to the Romans and their destruction of the Temple and Jerusalem in AD 70. Therefore, if the people of the future prince were Romans, then it is a logical conclusion the prince in question must also be Roman or indicative of the peoples that destroyed the temple in AD 70 (Illustration 3).

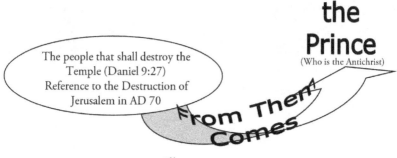

Illustration 3

We can also surmise that "the prince" in that passage has reference not to just any prince, but to a specific one; otherwise the writer would not have used the definite article *the.* Based on these facts, we can safely infer the prince Daniel had in mind is the Antichrist. In addition, we see two important facts about him in that one phrase alone:

- He will be of European (Rome) descent.
- He will be a prince or ruler.

The reason for all this is to point out the seven heads of the beast in Revelation seventeen have a dual interpretation—seven kings and seven hills (Revelation 17:8–10). I don't think there is any debate about the symbolism of the seven heads as hills and their being representative of the city of Rome's geographic location. The more difficult question is, how are we to understand their analogy to kings? I believe the answer lies in the language itself. John has already been told earlier in the seventeenth chapter of Revelation that five of these kings have fallen or no longer exist. By this, the angel cannot have in mind fallen empires that existed before John; the language will not allow it. For example, in verse twelve of the seventeen chapter of Revelation where the angel interprets the heads as kings, the Greek word *basileus* (bas-il-yooce) is used. This word means "a monarch, or king."[1] In every other instance where this word is used in Revelation seventeen, it is from the same Greek word *basileus*. Therefore, we must infer that it refers to literal kings. As far as their identity goes, God chose not to reveal them to us through the angel. As is the case in much of Revelation, where Scripture is silent or does not lend any information for proper interpretation, this writer remains silent as well.

What we can surmise however is the first five are no longer on the scene at the time John received the revelation. The sixth one or the *"one that is"* obviously refers to Domitian, the ruler of Rome during the time of John's exile. After these rulers move off the world's stage, there will arise a seventh and eighth king. The phrase *"even he is the eighth, and is of the seventh"* seems to be the angel's way of stressing that the eighth king is not really a different person, but somehow is identical with the seventh king (Illustration 4).

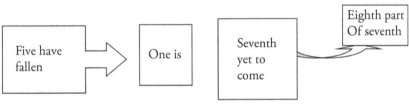

Illustration 4

This explanation by the angel of the seventh and eighth king appears to be a contradiction, since something cannot exist and not exist at the same time. To understand what he means by this, we must examine it with verse three of the thirteenth chapter of Revelation. In that particular passage, we read of an odd occurrence. One of the

---

[1] Zodhiates, Spiros, *The Hebrew-Greek Key Study Bible: King James Version* (AMG Publishers, 1984).

beast's heads receives a mortal wound. What this statement suggests is that seemingly one of the seven heads of the beast is killed. Having already concluded the seventh head is symbolic of the Antichrist; we can conclude that this is the head fatally wounded.

Based on this, the following inference can be drawn from the angel's explanation about the seventh and eighth head. During the first half of the Antichrist's reign, the world will enjoy peace and prosperity and is indicative of his appearance as a conquering king riding on a white horse with a bow but no arrows. However, at the midpoint of his reign, he will either experience an assassination attempt or be killed and somehow undergoes some sort of a resurrection. I must stress here that this is solely an inference on the writer's part. However, I do believe based on the rest of chapter thirteen, Satan seemingly convinces the world that something miraculous has happened to this man. So convincing is his deception the whole world will worship the Antichrist, who from this point on becomes known as the Beast. This and the information provided in the rest of chapter seventeen explains why the Bible presents Antichrist in the sixth chapter of Revelation already wearing a king's crown and as the eighth king.

Another important piece of information given to us in the thirteenth chapter of Revelation is in regard to the Antichrist's power. First, we find that it comes from the dragon or Satan. I gather from John's remarks Satan did not give up on his quest to dominate the world through a human being. He was unsuccessful in his first attempt to gain control of the world through the man Jesus (Matthew 4:1–11). However, he will seemingly succeed the next time he makes that same offer to the man who will eventually become known as "The Beast." Because of his acceptance of Satan's offer, he will have rulership and authority over every nation in the world. Scripture is clear that Satan is the Prince of this world (John 12:31), the father of all unbelievers (John 8:44), and the Prince of the Powers of the air (Ephesians 2:2). Furthermore, the offer made to Jesus during the Wilderness Temptation is enough evidence that God has given the kingdoms of the world to him (for a time) to do with them as he pleases. Therefore, the Antichrist, who will be Satan's man on earth, will easily ride into the hearts and minds of people through deception and trickery. The world is so eager today for peace that it's easy to see how such a man will be able to gain the people's loyalty and reverence. This particular trait of the Antichrist is also brought out in the eighth verse of the seventh chapter of Daniel and further points out the interrelationship between Daniel and Revelation.

Though Satan gives the Antichrist his powers, chapter seventeen rightly tells us that "God hath put in their hearts to fulfill His will, and to agree, and give their kingdom unto the beast, until the words of God shall be fulfilled" (Revelation 17:17). This verse assures us that all the things (including the other kings surrender of their own power), which take place during this time, are part of God's sovereign and providential plan. It also gives us proper perspective about Satan and the power he has. We must never see him as some rogue angelic being in the spirit realm having free reign to do as he pleases. His power, though real, is limited by the all-powerful hand and will of God. So as world leaders willingly yield their power to the Beast, Christians who will be alive at that time will be able to stand strong with hope as their anchor because of their knowledge that God is still in control.

CHAPTER 9

THE RESTRAINER

And ye know what withholdeth that he
might revealed in his time.
—2 Thessalonians 2:6

After presenting a chronology of events that must precede the coming of Christ, Paul explains or rather reminds the Thessalonian Christians the reason the Antichrist has not yet come is because the restrainer holds him back (2 Thessalonians 2:5–6). The way Paul phrases his statement implies that this was a well-known fact to them. In making such a definitive statement, he seems to be saying, "You know very well who this restrainer is." Here lies the difficulty in interpreting this particular passage. As stated before, Paul must have done extensive teaching in Thessalonica on the last days. Unfortunately, Scripture does not provide a record of what he taught. Therefore, this passage, as well as others like it, must be interpreted with other Scripture, and not theories. One thing that is agreeable by all about this passage is that whoever the restrainer is, he has to be more powerful than Satan.

So what does the Scripture have to say about the identity of the restrainer? This particular passage in Paul's second letter to the church at Thessalonica is the only reference to a restrainer in the sense of holding back the Antichrist's appearance. Based on the context of 2 Thessalonians 2:6–7, we know that he cannot be a created being. It also eliminates principles of nature, seen or unseen, such as the forces of good over evil, or light over darkness. When these possibilities are eliminated, the only other logical conclusion left is the three Persons of the Trinity.

In light of the latter conclusion, most theologians have resolved themselves to conclude the restrainer has to be the Holy Spirit. This does sound logical, since God the Father and God the Son sent Him to indwell Christians. Through His power, we are able to overcome evil and sin in our lives (1 John 4:4). Through Him, we are able to minister and proclaim the gospel message to the world, and it is His regenerative and quickening power that rescues sinners from a world of darkness and sin into God's marvelous light (Ephesians 2:1–3; 1 Peter 2:9). Also, one of His ministries is the convicting of sin, righteousness, and judgment (cf. John 16:8). With all these Scriptural evidences of His role both in the believer and unbeliever, it would be difficult to deny His role as the restrainer of evil as well. Here lies the question—does the Scripture support such a view?

Our first approach in answering these questions, is to first see whether Scripture supports the fact of the Holy Spirit being a restrainer of evil. The obvious place to start from is our Lord's own words recorded in the fourteenth chapter of John's gospel regarding the Holy Spirit's role. Notice what He said about the Holy Spirit and His coming into the world.

> But I tell you the truth: it is for your good that I am going away. Unless I go away, the Counselor will not come to you; but if I go, I will send you him to you. When He comes, he will convict the world of guilt in regard to sin and righteousness and judgment: in regard to righteousness, because I am going to the Father, where you can see me no longer; and in regards to judgment, because the prince of this world now stands condemned. But when He, the Spirit of truth, comes, He will guide you into all truth. He will not speak on His own; He will speak only

what he hears, and He will tell you what is yet to come. He will bring glory to me. (John 16:7–11, 13–14 KJV)

This passage reveals specific works or ministries that are uniquely those of the Holy Spirit. Obviously, these are not the only works that He does in the lives of believer and unbeliever alike. Other portions of the New Testament bear this out and lists other functions performed by Him that are equally important in edifying and equipping the body of Jesus Christ. However, I would like to restrict this discussion to the role (not His gifts or role in salvation) of the Holy Spirit in the world, especially His dealing with evil. If "He" is the restrainer of evil; then our Lord would have said so in his final words on earth.

First, Jesus points out the Holy Spirit will be our Comforter. This would have been reassuring and consoling to the disciples as Jesus prepared them for His departure. During the last three years, their lives had been a major part of His and He a major part of theirs. He had been their constant companion and friend, feeding them with His words, teaching them about heavenly matters. But now He tells them that He must go away in order that the Comforter might come and be with them. The word used for Comforter comes from the Greek word *parakletos* (par-ak-lay-tos). Some bibles translate it as Advocate, Helper, or Counselor. The meaning of these words accurately portray the role of the Holy Spirit in the believer's life. In times of distress, He comes alongside to empower us so we will be able to endure and stand during times of trials and persecution. In like manner, the Holy Spirit is our companion who comes alongside us to give aid, help, spiritual strength, and wisdom in our daily walk. He is the One who comes alongside to provide help not possible by any other person.

Second, and more important to this discussion, is our Lord's emphasis on the Spirit's role in the world. He states that His main role will be that of convincing or convicting. This would take place in three areas. First, He will convince or reprove the world of sin. In the Bible, *world* means more than the planet Earth. In Scripture, it is also the word used when talking about or referring to the world systems. When used in the latter sense, it refers to the governmental, economical, and social structure of the physical world we live in.

However, Christ's use of it in this passage has in mind the sum total of man in sin, or all people who are not Christians. Therefore, the Holy Spirit must first "convict (reprove) the world of guilt." This unique work of the Holy Spirit is the only way man can realize his condition is one that separates him from God and His goodness. The word *convict* in Greek means "to convince." It is a legal term and carries the idea of a prosecutor cross-examining a person on trial, presenting to him and the jury undeniable facts and evidences of his obvious guilt. This evidence is so complete and thorough that the only possible verdict from a reasonable and fair jury is one of guilty. This is what the Holy Spirit does in the heart and mind of the unsaved. He first gives them a new heart and a new disposition toward God and His word. This process is called regeneration. When faced with the evidences of his sin, guilt, and ungodliness, his or her regenerated heart convicts them to the point where they fall before the Supreme Judge and plead for mercy and forgiveness.

The work of convicting sinners of who they are before God is one of the most important roles of the Holy Spirit. He convinced us by the gospel that we were sinners, depraved and unable to save our self, and that we need a Savior in the worst way! This, combined with the gift of faith, enabled us to respond to the call of God on our life. Despite what the world may believe about all roads leading to Heaven, Scripture is clear there is only one way—Jesus Christ (John 14:6; Acts 4:12). Whenever man says and believes that he is good enough to appear before a righteous God in his present condition, he has rejected God's clear declaration of his sinful state. As a result, he remains under God's condemnation. Because God is just and righteous, all who refuse to accept His way of salvation will eventually suffer His wrath, judgment, and punishment. He has given the world His only Son—Jesus Christ—as the only means of satisfying the penalty and requirements of His law. God has promised that whoever accepts Him and his redemptive work will live with him forever (John 3:16). On the other hand, those who reject Him will suffer eternally in the lake of fire (John 3:18).

Not only does the Holy Spirit convince the world of sin, but He also convinces the world of righteousness. Again this refers to Christ's character, mainly that He is the righteous One sent from God. The biggest problem the religious leaders had with Jesus was that He made Himself equal to God. To them, this was the ultimate sin. He agitated them further by declaring that after His death, God would raise Him (Acts 13:30) from the dead, and He would ascend to His Father. They saw this as being the ultimate blasphemy and further fueled their hatred of Him.

On the Day of Pentecost, the Holy Spirit speaking through the apostle Peter affirmed the righteousness of Christ with the words "Jesus of Nazareth, a man approved of God among you by miracles and wonders and signs, which God did by Him in the midst of you" (Acts 2:22 KJV). In making this statement, Peter was saying the works that Jesus did proved His righteousness before God. They were the validating seal of God that He was of and from Him! Based on all Christ did, the Jewish leaders had no valid reason for not believing that He was the promised Messiah. This is why the Hebrew writer puts before all men the question, "How can we neglect so great a salvation?" especially because of the convincing work of the Spirit.

Lastly, the Holy Spirit will convict the world of judgment. Regardless of their beliefs about God, the Bible, and sin, the fact remains that all unbelievers are under the dominion of Satan, the Prince of this world. In reality, they are citizens of his kingdom. While it's true that they do get to enjoy all the things his kingdom has to offer, that joy is meaningless and short when compared with an eternity of suffering and pain awaiting all unbelievers who reject Christ. The cars, fine jewelry, parties, and luxuries are theirs, but only while they live in this earthly realm. There is a final judgment coming where all men will have to appear before the righteous Judge and give an account of their deeds while on earth. Most people regard Jesus as being a good man who went about teaching and preaching peace and love. However, the New Testament stresses that He also spoke of the reality of a real God and His coming judgment on the world.

When Christ rose from the grave, He conquered death, and God judged Satan. Although his judgment was not immediate, since he still exercises limited control over this world, his kingdom nevertheless received a deadly blow. Until that point, he had free reign through the power of sin and death. There was no way for man to defeat him, no way of ever overcoming his power and influence in their lives. Because Christ has conquered death and Satan, Christians are free from Satan's power and influence. This does not mean that Christians will never sin, instead it means their disposition is now one that hates sin. Before, they loved sin and therefore, were at the mercy of Satan who uses sin as the means of causing both saint and sinner to continue to live a life displeasing to God. Now, the Christian can resist him and the desire to sin by the power of the Holy Spirit and God's word. This is how God judged Satan: He took away the hold he had over humanity since Adam sinned in the Garden of Eden. Although it is only partially complete, the Holy Spirit works in the hearts of Christians, convincing us that God does judge evil, and that evil will not ultimately overcome righteousness. He lets man know that one day, God will cast Satan into the lake of fire and all those who have rejected the only begotten Son of God the Father.

As stated earlier, these are not the only works of the Holy Spirit. The reason for mentioning these specific ones is to discover whether we should regard Him as being the restrainer mentioned by Paul in his letter to the Thessalonian Christians. Based on what has been said so far, it would seem that if He does restrain evil, it is evil within the life of the believer (by convicting us when we sin) and not the world. I would further state, though not dogmatically, that I do not believe that Scripture teaches the Holy Spirit is the restrainer that is holding back the Antichrist.

Those accepting the view that the Holy Spirit is the restrainer are faced with even more difficult questions to answer. For example, those who teach this view also teach that when the restrainer (the Holy Spirit) is removed, both He and the church are taken out of the world. If this is true, it becomes difficult to understand, let alone explain, how these same teachers insist there will be a great revival during the tribulation period. Scripture makes it clear that left to himself, man will never accept God until he has been regenerated and made spiritually alive by the Holy Spirit (Ephesians 2:1, 5).

In response to this obvious obstacle, we're told the "tribulation saints" will be saved in the same manner as the Old Testament saints were. It is true the Spirit did act or come upon Old Testament saints. However, His role then was one of empowering men and women of God to perform specific ministries or works through Him. To say God set them apart in a manner that did not directly involve the Holy Spirit would be unscriptural. We see evidence of this in Samson's life when he tried to defeat the Philistines after Delilah cut his hair. The loss of his strength was not only linked to his hair being cut but, more importantly, it was the fact that the Holy Spirit had left him (Judges 16:20). David understood this truth as well and prayed that God not take His Spirit from him (Psalm 51:11). Paul brings out this same point when explaining justification in the fourth chapter of Romans. His main theme was that faith alone justifies man and not works. To establish his point, he uses Abraham as the prime example that his faith in God justified him and not his works (cf. Romans 4:1–4). This one statement alone by Paul confirms Old Testament saints were saved just as we are—justification by faith alone.

During His conversation with Nicodemus, Jesus made it plain to him that "unless a man is born of water and the spirit, he can not enter the kingdom of heaven" (John 3:3,5 KJV). Therefore, if the tribulation saints are "saints" at all, it has to be through the indwelling power of the Holy Spirit.

Another question that is just as important is that of determining the qualifications that will be used in deciding who will take part in this first Rapture and who will be left behind. Consider for a moment Paul's statement in his first epistle to the Corinthians, "for by one Spirit are we all baptized into one body, whether we be Jews or Gentiles, whether we be bond or free; and have been all made to drink into one Spirit" (v. 13 KJV). Although Paul's main emphasis in this passage was on spiritual gifts, his point was that all the gifts, regardless of how small was necessary because we are one body. This means the body of Christ needs every Christian to be complete. Remove any one section, regardless of its insignificance, and the whole body itself becomes incomplete. Added to this is Paul's letter to the Roman Christians where he tells them that we have been baptized into Jesus Christ (Romans 6:3). He did not say that part of us are baptized, but all of us! The reason for bringing up these passages is to point out that Christians are nothing more than people who were part of the world at one point in their lives. However, at salvation, they are baptized and united in Christ and have become one body, one church and one bride (Illustration 1).

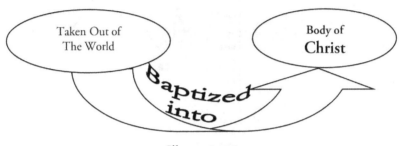

Illustration 1

It is inconceivable that anyone or any event could divide Christ's body (cf. Romans 8:35). We are "lively stones" says Peter in his first letter who are "built up a spiritual house" (1 Peter 2:5). The New Testament makes it clear that the death of Christ not only abolished the hostility that existed between God and man, but also has created in Himself one new man (Ephesians 2:14–16).

When God foreordained and formed the church in His mind, it was one united body. When describing the church, the Bible use such terms as *house, field, body, kingdom,* and *bride* because they all stress the singularity and unity that characterizes her. The major difference between Old Testament saints, pretribulation, and tribulation saints is that they lived during different ages in history. Any other distinctions, such as those Christians living before the tribulation period who are found watchful being raptured secretly while others remain and go through that period (Illustration 2) is difficult to be supported by Scripture.

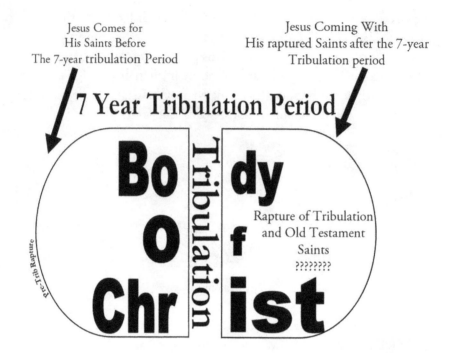

Illustration 2

Whether we are Old, New, "pre-" or "post-" tribulation saints, we will all be raptured at the same time since the Body or Bride of Christ cannot be separated. This "oneness" that characterizes the Body of Christ is one of the foundational doctrine of our faith. Anyone who doubts the significance and essential nature of this teaching need only examine our Lord's High Priestly Prayer. In verses six straight through the end of the seventeenth chapter of John's gospel, Jesus pours out His heart to the Father on our behalf. His earnest desire is that we be one as He and the Father are one.

The illustrations above clearly point out the danger of putting forth the idea that part of the Body of Christ is raptured before the tribulation while the other half is raptured after it. Add to this the belief the Holy Spirit (being the restrainer) is also removed from the world before the beginning of the seven-year tribulation period (Daniel's Seventieth Week), and what you have is a theological nightmare. This is especially true when this teaching is placed against scriptures that clearly teach that Christians will be alive during that period (cf. Daniel 7:21; Revelation 6:11; 13:7). The immediate questions that comes to mind are: how will they be comforted, guided, and kept, and even more importantly, how were they regenerated (cf. John. 3:3; Philippians. 1:6)? It's unimaginable that God the Father would leave His children without the promised Helper during such a hellish time on earth, especially in light of Christ's own promises to us (cf. John 14:16, 18; 16:7).

Besides this, consider the apostle Paul's teaching to the Christians at Thessalonica about those who had already died. Notice his response to their concern, "For this we say unto you by the word of the Lord, that we which are alive and remain unto the coming of the Lord shall not prevent them which are asleep. For the Lord himself shall descend from heaven with a shout, with the voice of the archangel, and with the trump of God: and the dead in Christ shall rise first: Then we which are alive and remain shall be caught up together with them in the clouds to meet the Lord in the air" (1 Thessalonians 4:15–17a KJV). In this passage, Paul emphatically states that those of us who are alive will not prevent (go ahead of) those that are asleep. Any serious exegetical study of this passage would clearly reveal he has a onetime event in mind.

The reason for bringing up these particular passages of Scriptures is to point out the difficulty in accepting or putting forth the current position that the identity of the restrainer is the Holy Spirit, and that the church will be raptured before the tribulation's period. As stated earlier, Scripture makes it clear that Christians will be martyred during the tribulation period (Revelation 6:9). This means that they would have died after the Rapture. Were they not saints? If they were, how did the Rapture take place without them? Was Paul's teaching to the Thessalonians in error? He distinctly stated the "dead in Christ" would be raised first, and then, those of us who are blessed to be alive during that period would follow them. At no point in his teaching does he mention a second rapture, which of necessity must take place to account for those who died and are martyred during the tribulation period. To further complicate matters, it would also call for a Third Coming of Christ: one at the beginning of the Tribulation

Period and another one at the end or some other time. A teaching found neither in the Old or New Testament (cf. Acts 1:11).

These facts alone raise serious doubts in this writer's mind that the restrainer is the Holy Spirit. Perhaps the answer to this question can be found in other writings of Paul. For example, in speaking about those who chose to live a life in rebellion to God's Law, Paul in the first chapter of Romans tells us that God "gave them up to uncleanness through the lusts of their own heart" (Romans 1:24 NKJV). Based on this statement, I believe Paul, if not providing the answer, is pointing to the possibility that God the Father is the restrainer.

We know that if God were to release his control over evil, this world would not be a pleasant place to live. But according to Paul's letter to the Romans, that's exactly what He does. What men fail to realize about God's long-suffering in punishing sin is that He does so because it is to show His mercy, with the express purpose of bringing them to repentance. However, when men reject and despise this goodness, God gives them over to fulfill the lusts of their flesh. Paul tells Timothy that, in the last days "evil men and seducers shall wax worse and worse, deceiving and being deceived" (2 Timothy 3:13). The senseless acts of violence and the prideful attitude of man are the direct result of God's hand being removed from them. All one has to do is just pick up the daily newspaper or turn on the local television and see that immorality has crossed boundaries never before seen in this country. To put it another way, the restraint on evil is slowly being removed and is a sure sign the Lord's Coming is drawing near. Who is the restrainer in this passage? If it's God in the Roman's passage, then maybe He's also the subject in Paul's letter to the Thessalonians. However, even with these and other passages, no definite evidence can be given that would point to the Holy Spirit as the restrainer.

The fact is the only persons who clearly knew the identity of the restrainer were the Christians at Thessalonica and Paul. Since God chose not to reveal to us his identity, extreme care should be taken in interpreting this verse as proof the Holy Spirit is the restrainer. When I look at the evil in this world, it is enough for me to know that it is being restrained, that it does have its limit. More importantly, we should rest in the assurance that Satan does not have control over this world. Instead he has been given permission to rule for a time and his man (Antichrist) cannot come until the Persons of the Godhead allow him.

CHAPTER 10

DANIEL'S SEVENTY WEEKS

Seventy weeks are determined upon thy
people and upon thy holy city.

—Daniel 9:24

The purpose in talking about the world empires and the rise of the Antichrist in the previous chapters was to point out that God has revealed to His people not only His will about salvation but the future as well. In making this statement, this writer is not implying that we can know and understand all that God is doing in the world. Not only would that be arrogant and foolish on my part, but unscriptural as well. However, for anyone to say or believe that God has not revealed to us certain specifics about Christ's Second Coming with the purpose of preparing us for it is just as unscriptural. Jesus told His disciples that when the Spirit comes, "He will show you things to come" (John 16:13). Jesus directed this promise to the apostles specifically and generally to all Christians. What I mean is that, in this particular statement made by Jesus, He stressed to the disciples the Holy Spirit would speak through them or inspire them to write the New Testament which contain things about the future. Just as the Holy Spirit revealed to the apostles the things of the future so they could write them down for us in the New Testament, He also shed light on those same truths so we can understand them. After all, the church is built upon the teachings of the prophets and apostles (Ephesians 2:20).

I explained all of this to say we go to great lengths to stress that no one knows the day or hour when our Lord will return, which I believe to be true. However, when this statement of fact is made, it should always be done qualitatively. By this, I mean it should not be made in isolation from all other supporting scriptures that expound on it. For example, Matthew 24:36 and Mark 13:32 are used as supporting scriptures most of the time when this statement is made. However, seldom do these same proponents point out that Jesus made both statements in His humanity, and should not be interpreted apart from Acts 1:7. In the Acts passage, we clearly see Christ in His glorified body implicitly saying this knowledge is no longer hidden from Him. As the God-Man, Jesus never stopped being God the Son while on earth. He was just as much God then as He ever was and is now. But by the same token, he was just as much man as you and I are—experiencing the same pains, emotions, and limitations as any finite creature. So when He said that he did not know the day or hour of His return, He was speaking from the standpoint of His humanity. Such knowledge is beyond the scope of our human mind as it was His and could not be known without the Divine assistance of God (cf. Matthew 16:17). While this was true of the man Jesus, it is not true of God the Son because He is fully God, coequal and coeternal with the other two Persons of the Godhead. While it is difficult to grasp this truth, we must believe it; as it is one of the essential doctrines of the Christian Faith (1 John 4:3).

During the fourth century, a priest named Arius put forth the teaching that denied the Divinity of Jesus. He believed and taught that although Jesus was eternal, He was nevertheless a created being (though of the highest order), and therefore, there was a time when He did not exist. This teaching, which became known as Arianism, added fuel to an already burning fire of controversy that plagued the church then. To restore unity, Emperor Constantine convened an ecumenical council in AD 325. It was doing this council that a small group of Orthodox bishops successfully defended the doctrine of the Deity of Christ. Of particular note is the fact that the most ardent defender of this truth was a man named Athanasius, the secretary to Alexander, the bishop of Alexandria Egypt. The Nicene Creed was the result of this great council, which declared Jesus Christ to be "very God of very God, begotten, not made, being of one substance with the Father."[1] Therefore, those who would say there was a time when anything was hidden or unknown by Christ while on earth would make Him just another prophet or rabbi and add credence to the Arian heresy. In doing so, this writer believes He becomes no more than the Jesus of the Jehovah Witnesses, the Mormons, Muslims, and ultimately the world—just another good man who lived a perfect life. I would add, if this is the case, then we are all still in our sin for only God the Son could die to redeem man.

The reason for saying all this is to point out that while on earth, Jesus was the Rabbi. However, now that He has gone back to be with His Father, He has not stopped teaching us since He lives within us (John 17:23). This teaching is not limited just to salvation, but also the things to come as well. So even though we do not know the day or hour of His second coming, the Bible provides enough information about the events and signs that helps us know when Christ's Second Coming is near. I strongly believe Scripture tells us there will be a generation of Christians who will experience the most terrible time of persecution the world has ever known. Jesus stressed that God will shorten this period of time for the sake of those Christians. If He does not do so, no one would survive. The generation living when this period begins needs to be aware of the signs that will usher in this time frame and the Second Coming of Christ.

To achieve this purpose, the Bible provides a passage of Scripture recorded in the last four verses of the ninth chapter of Daniel; commonly referred to in Eschatology as "Daniel Seventy Weeks." Any meaningful discussion involving the final days of this world must of necessity include this teaching. The failure to read and understand this and other portions of Daniel makes it impossible to grasp and understand all other prophetic passages dealing with the last days, especially the book of Revelation. Although this period of time

---

[1]   The Nicene Creed

is more directly tied to God's judgment of Israel, we will discover during the course of our discussion that the whole world will be affected in one way or another.

If this period is so important, the obvious question becomes "How will we know when it is upon us?" Before we answer that question, I should point out the term *Seventy Weeks* did not originate with Daniel, but with the angel Gabriel (Daniel 9:24). It is that specific time in history when God will consummate His plan not only for Israel, but also the church, Satan, and sinners as well. Having said that, let us examine this time frame in more detail.

As stated earlier, we find this period of time recorded in the ninth chapter of the Old Testament Book of Daniel. The first half of that chapter is Daniel's prayer of adoration, supplication, and intercession to God for his people. In the twenty-first and twenty-second verse, the angel Gabriel tells him God had sent him. His mission was to give Daniel "skill and understanding" about his concern for his people. It is at this point that he tells him that "Seventy weeks are determined upon thy people and upon thy holy city, to finish the transgression, and to make an end of sins, and to make reconciliation for iniquity, and to bring in everlasting righteousness, and to seal up the vision and prophecy, and to anoint the most Holy" (Daniel 9:24 KJV).

Before we can understand Gabriel's message, we must examine the Hebrew word *shavua* (shaw-boo-ah) translated in this passage as *weeks*. When we think of weeks, seven days are in mind. However, in the language of the Jews, which would have been Daniel's immediate audience, it simply meant "seven," much like our word *dozen* or *gross*. According to Dr. McClain, "this Biblical 'weeks' of years was just as familiar to the Jew as the 'weeks' of days" (*Daniel's Prophecy of the 70 Weeks*, Dr. Alva J. McClain, Zondervan Publishing House).

Therefore, for us to get the correct meaning of these weeks, the context must be examined. In other words, if someone were to offer me a dozen of something, I would first have to know what the dozen consisted of (that is eggs, doughnuts, etc.) before I could give a proper response. In the passage under consideration, we must use the same process if we are to understand the meaning of the term *weeks*.

At the beginning of chapter nine, Daniel is reading the prophecy of Jeremiah, which dealt with the length of time the Jews would be held in Babylonian captivity. Based on this reading Daniel was able to understand the time frame God had set aside for the captivity of his people would be seventy years (Daniel 9:2–3). Since the prophecy was speaking in years, it is unthinkable that this same meaning would not continue throughout the context. The tenth chapter of Daniel further supports the conclusion that years are in view and not days. Examining these two chapters together is especially important in understanding this nonspecific term because he uses the same Hebrew word for weeks in the second and third verses of chapter ten. In those verses, it is clear that based on the context, he has to be talking about weeks of days, since Daniel is said to have been fasting for three weeks. The angel's response to Daniel in verses twelve and thirteen of that same chapter, further support the fact these were regular weeks of days. Notice that he explains the reason for his delay in responding to Daniel's prayer was because of a battle with the demonic being in charge of Persia; which lasted for twenty-one days. The twenty-one days is not so much the focal point as is the fact that God sent him "the first day" (v. 12a) that Daniel set his mind on understanding the vision. Therefore, it is easy to use the angel's response as a reference point to determine that Daniel had been fasting for twenty-one days or three weeks. Besides, it would be difficult to imagine anyone fasting or not anointing (that is applying lotion or oils) themselves for any period longer than three weeks of days in that region of the world (modern-day Iraq). Therefore, the Seventy Weeks in chapter nine are seventy weeks of years or 70 x 7 or 490 years (MacArthur, John, *John MacArthur's Bible Studies, The Future of Israel,* The Moody Bible Institute of Chicago), because Daniel was already thinking in years.

The next critical key word in this prophecy is the Hebrew word *chathak* (khaw-thak) translated as "determined" in verse twenty-four. Unlike its use in other sections of Daniel (Daniel 9:26, 27; 11:36), the meaning in this verse is to "cut off" or to cut out a portion of time. In a sense, God in His sovereignty looked down the portals of time and cut off a section of it, during which He would carry out six specific purposes for His people and Jerusalem. The fact that this time frame has Israel as its focus is unquestionable because Gabriel as much as says so in his interpretation that "Seventy weeks are determined upon thy people." Since he's talking to Daniel, the reference to "thy people" can have no other reference than the Jews. Notice the six things that God will carry out during this specific period of time. He will

- finish transgressions;
- make an end to sins;
- make reconciliation for iniquity;
- bring in everlasting righteousness;
- seal up visions and prophecy; and
- anoint the most holy.

A careful study of these actions by God reveals the first three were completed during Christ's First Coming while the latter three will be completed during His Second Coming. Having said that, let's examine the first three actions originated by God and completed by Christ.

The first things alluded to in the first coming of Christ is the fact that He would "finish transgressions." A better translation of the Hebrew word used for *finish* in this passage is "shut up" or "restrained." In the sixth chapter of the Old Testament book of I Samuel, the same Hebrew word for *finish* is used (1 Samuel 6:10). There, the writer used it to explain that while the mother cows hauled the Ark of the Covenant back to Israel, their calves were shut up. When looked at from that perspective, we see before us the idea of a fixed or set boundary. This is exactly what happened to sin at Calvary and the empty tomb. Up to that point, the Law had energized sin (Romans 7:5). The Law not only energized sin but exposed sin for what it is. It also drove us to sin even more. We all have experienced this principle when, for years, we have walked around a patch of ground until the owner puts a sign "Do Not Walk on the Grass." The moment the sign is seen, an inner urge swells up inside of us, driving us to do what we know to be wrong. That was man's problem from the moment Adam sinned. No matter how he tried to obey the Law, he always fell short, either in action or thought. However, Christ fulfilled the requirements of the Law by His perfect obedience to it (Matthew 5:17). He followed and obeyed all God's laws, both internally (in thoughts, thinking, motive) and externally (living right before men and God).

Not only was it necessary that the Law be fulfilled in that way, but the penalty for disobeying God's law is death. It is impossible for any person who has ever lived to pay this penalty due to the sin nature that dwells within each of us. Therefore, a substitute—one sinless and undefiled—must do it for us. Jesus Christ became our substitute and died for us on the cross. In doing so, He endured God's wrath and punishment on our behalf (2 Corinthians 5:21). But if that was all Christ had done for us, we would still not be free because of death's reign. Sin is death's sting, according to Paul in the fifteenth chapter of his first letter to the Corinthians. He personifies death to stress its power over us, both physically and spiritually. As the scorpion's power lies within the sting of his tail, so death separates man by its sting—sin. This is why the resurrection was necessary. Without it, death kept its sting and would have remained a barrier between God and man. Christ's resurrection was the confirmation that all aspects of sin had been defeated, including death. Paul picks up on this theme in the fifth chapter of Romans by stating, "as sin hath reigned unto death, even so might grace reign through righteousness unto eternal life by Jesus Christ our Lord" (Romans 5:21 KJV). This is the shutting up, the restraining of sin as God pours His grace upon the elect through the work of His Son. No longer does sin and death have a free reign in the world; it has now been "shut up, restrained!"

But not only will He finish transgressions, He will also make an "end to sin." Again, we must be careful in our interpretation of this phrase as well, since sin is still present, even in Christians. In the margin of the New King James Version, this term is translated as "to seal up" which offers a better explanation or understanding of it. Whenever something is sealed up, such as a package or a chest, its content is hidden from view. That was what happened when Jesus Christ died on the cross.

On that dark day, He became the scapegoat for everyone who accepts Him as their Lord and Savior. In doing so, He not only bore their sins, He also took them away from God's presence. Now when the Father sees us, He does not see our sins because they have been sealed up, covered by the blood of His Son. So thorough is this sealing that God declares through the prophet Isaiah that He "blotteth out thy transgressions for mine own sake, and will not remember thy sins" (Isaiah 43:25 KJV).

The third thing that Christ will do during His first coming is to make reconciliation for sins. The meaning of the word *reconciliation* is "to cover." This word suggests to us the propitiatory work of Christ. By His death and suffering, He satisfied the righteous requirements of the law and the penalty of sin. In doing so, he provided the only means by which God could pardon and forgive us of our sins. God the Father was now appeased. Even though in the Old Testament, sacrifices were made yearly to atone for sin, this did nothing other than to provide a temporary covering of sin. Even the act itself was only symbolic and a shadow of Christ's ultimate sacrifice (cf. Hebrews 10:1–6). The Hebrew writer brings out the insufficiency of the Old Testament sacrifices in his statement, "In burnt offerings and sacrifices for sin thou hast had no pleasure" (Hebrews 10:6 KJV). He was not saying that God had no pleasure in the people performing the act, since they were only doing as He had commanded. His displeasure was in the fact the blood of goats and bulls had no power to redeem the eternal soul of man, and therefore could not achieve its intended purpose. Therefore, Christ's first coming and subsequent death, burial, and resurrection fulfilled the first three purposes of the Seventy Weeks—to restrain, seal, and cover sin.

But what of the remaining three purposes listed in the Seventy Weeks? As stated earlier, all six acts comprise Christ's first and second coming. Having determined the first three belonged to His first appearance, the last three must belong to His second. The phrase *to bring in* points this out and introduces the fourth act. It suggests that at some point, Jesus Christ will bring an everlasting righteousness into the world. Since Adam's first sin of disobedience, man has failed in all his attempts to be righteous before God. This is especially true during these latter days. Therefore, this fact alone lends credence to the fact that some future time must be in view.

The fifth act mentioned in this prophecy is the sealing up of prophecy and visions. We can conclude from the previous discussion on the word *seal* that fulfillment of this act involves the shutting up of the prophecies and visions. In other words, we can study, read, and properly interpret prophecy as it relates to the last days and the Second Coming. However, when Christ returns, there will be no further need for prophecies or visions, because they all find fulfillment in His First and Second Coming. They will be shut up forever.

The final act involves anointing "the most holy." This term is specific and always refers to the inner sanctuary of the Tabernacle and Temple—the Holy of Holies. Although some use this phrase as a reference to the whole temple or of Jerusalem, its most common use in scripture is always that of the Holy of Holies (cf. Exodus 26:33–34; 29:37; 30:29, 36) and Daniel would have understood it in this way. The other and perhaps most important key to understanding the intended meaning of this phrase is to understand the term *anoint* was used of consecrating or setting aside either a person or an object for use by God. Therefore, kings, priest, and prophets were anointed and set apart from their countrymen to perform a specific service for God (cf. Exodus 28:41; 40:15; 1 Kings 19:16; 1 Samuel 10:1; 15:1). The normal means or instrument of anointing was oil. However, in the Daniel's passage the means of anointing will not be oil but a person—Jesus Christ, the Messiah, the Anointed One. In the Jewish mind, there is and remains no greater means of consecration than that of having the Messiah Himself anoint or consecrate the holiest of all Jewish structures.

Since the first temple was destroyed by the Babylonians, and the second one by the Romans, the Jews have longed for the appearance of the Promised Messiah. They believed that when He comes, He will bring back to Israel the glory that characterized the Davidic Kingdom. As pointed out earlier, this was not His intended purpose during His first appearance, but will be when He comes back the second time. Not only will He anoint the Holy of Holies and restore Israel as the central point of worship, but will also bring everlasting righteousness and seal up all visions and prophecies.

Lastly, according to the thirty-ninth chapter of Ezekiel, there will be a fourth Temple (the third[1] one will be rebuilt during the tribulation period) rebuilt during the millennial reign of Christ. His prophecy adds further evidence the last three of the six acts mentioned in Daniel nine have yet to be fulfilled.

---

[1] The first temple was the temple of Solomon. The second one is regarded as Herod's Temple, but is more appropriately understood as the Temple that was rebuilt by Zerubbabel after the Babylonian and Persian Captivity.

CHAPTER 11

THE UNFOLDING OF THE SEVENTY WEEKS

Seventy weeks are determined…

Having concluded in the previous chapter that the Seventy Weeks have specific purposes and designs for the nation of Israel, we will now examine this time frame to find out, as best as possible, how it will be played out. Below is a diagram of how I believe we are to understand its relationship to human history as a whole.

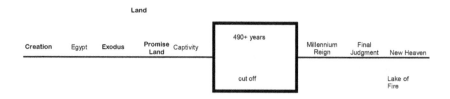

Although not obvious from the illustration, the time frame under discussion is more than 490 years. We will see why this has to be the case as we examine this time frame more closely later. But before we can look at the details of the Seventy Weeks, we must determine its starting point. After all, the prophecy would be of little value to anyone if there were no way of knowing when it started. Daniel seemingly had this same question in mind after receiving the prophecy. However, before he had a chance to ask, the angel Gabriel told him that it would start with "the decree to restore and rebuild Jerusalem." According to this portion of the passage, the prophecy would start when the decree goes forth to rebuild the city and walls of Jerusalem. Another important aspect about the building process is that it would be accomplished under tremendous opposition or, as stated by the angel, during "troublous times."

But what decree is in view? The Bible records four such decrees: the decrees of Cyrus, Darius, and two by Artaxerxes. The decrees by Cyrus, Darius, and the first one by Artaxerxes only dealt with building the Temple. Also the building process was almost unimpeded. Therefore, we can omit these three decrees in favor of the second decree of Artaxerxes, recorded in the second chapter of the Old Testament Book of Nehemiah. Nehemiah was Artaxerxes's cupbearer. This gave him direct access to the king and made it possible for him to request permission from him to rebuild the city of Jerusalem, the walls around it, and gates (Nehemiah 2:5–8). Artaxerxes honored Nehemiah's request and gave him all the authority and permits needed to start the rebuilding.

When the building began, the Moabites, Ammonites, and Samaritans were angry with Nehemiah for this undertaking. So bad was their hostility that it became necessary to assign guards to him for protection. Also, the builders and other workers were ordered to work with their armor on and swords at their side. At strategic points were trumpeters with the express purpose of watching for the enemies that opposed the construction. These actions, as well as others, by the surrounding neighbors of the city confirmed what the angel had told Daniel that the wall and city would be built during "troublous times." These actions, both by Nehemiah and his enemies, confirm the fact this was the correct decree that started the Seventy Weeks.

Having fixed its starting point, all that's left now is to find out when it ends. According to the angel, sixty-nine weeks would expire from the time of Artaxerxes's decree until "the Messiah the Prince." By reading the twenty-sixth verse of Daniel chapter nine, we find there are two key events that will occur during the sixty-nine weeks (Illustration 1). First, there is the first seven weeks (forty-nine years). During this time, the people would rebuild the city and wall. Second, there is a sixty-two-week time span between building the city and the recognition of the Messiah as Prince and His subsequent death. The entire sixty-nine weeks ends, not at the death of Jesus, but when Israel recognize Jesus as their Messiah and Prince.

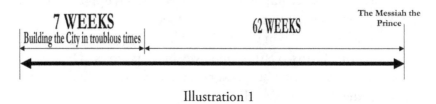

Illustration 1

Although there were many false messiahs before Jesus, none fulfilled the requirements of Daniel's prophecy as He did. Years before Daniel had received this message, both Isaiah and David (Psalm 22; Isaiah 53:1–12) had prophesied of the Messiah's suffering and death. And even if somehow those events could not be linked to Jesus as the Messiah, the means of His death should have been a dead giveaway that he was the person Daniel and the other prophets prophesied about. The angel brings this out in his use of the term *cut off.* The Hebrew word is *karath* (kaw-rath) and means "to destroy or consume." It is interesting that he would use such a strong word in speaking of the manner in which Jesus Christ would be killed. To better understand this term, perhaps it is good to look to others who have devoted much more time and energy to the study of this particular word than this writer. One such person is Dr. John MacArthur who states that, "*Karath* is used a number of times in the Old Testament to describe the execution of a criminal (Leviticus 7:20; Psalm 37:9; Proverbs 2:22). Daniel's use of the term implies the Messiah would die a criminal's death—a prophecy so specific, it seems incomprehensible that when Jesus was presented in triumph in precise accord with Daniel's timetable but then crucified, the Jewish people would not immediately recognize who He was" (Dr. John MacArthur, *John MacArthur Bible Studies, The Future of Israel, Daniel 9:20–12:13,* Moody Press). Based on this word (*karath*) and Dr. MacArthur's explanation of it, we see plainly that God revealed to Daniel the exact time frame for two of the most important events in human history—Jesus being proclaimed as Messiah and His subsequent death on the cross.

So then, the facts are clear that it is the second decree of Artaxerxes that started Daniel's Seventy Weeks. The city and its walls were completed during troublous times in seven of those seventy weeks. Sixty-two weeks after the rebuilding, Jesus of Nazareth rode into Jerusalem on a donkey. The people laid palm branches in His pathway and proclaimed Him as the Prince of Israel. As they went through this process, they had no idea they were fulfilling this prophecy. Recognizing their ignorance, Luke's comments that Jesus wept over their actions. They were oblivious to the true meaning of what they were doing (Luke 19:41–42).

But how do we know that Jesus's triumphant entry into Jerusalem was the point in time that ended the sixty-nine weeks? One of the gifted men of God who corroborated this down to the very day was Sir Robert Anderson. His book entitled *The Coming Prince* lays out this time frame with such accuracy that even skeptics are forced to (even though reluctantly), accept the preciseness of Daniel's prophecy of the sixty-nine weeks. Both Dr. John MacArthur[1] and Dr. Alva J. McClain[1] have summarized these calculations. In doing so, both authors single out the critical fact (as well as others), that the calculations must be done the way Jews would have understood time. Unlike our calendar, Jewish years consist of only 360 days, with no leap years. Also, the names and length of their months are different from ours. Therefore, when Nehemiah was enquiring of the king, the Spirit made it a point of stating that it was in the month of "Nisan" that Artaxerxes granted him his request (Nehemiah 2:1). The significance of mentioning this month by name (something not normally done) is brought out in the fact that according to Jewish historians, Nisan (March) is also the month when Jesus rode into Jerusalem. Since there was no date given in the Nehemiah passage, both Dr. MacArthur and Dr. McClain conclude that whenever a specific date

---

[1] John MacArthur, *John MacArthur's Bible Studies The Future of Israel: Daniel 9:20–12:13* (Chicago: Moody Press).

[1] Alva J. McClain, *Daniel's Prophecy of the 70 Weeks* (Grand Rapids: Zondervan Publishing House).

is not given, the first day of the month is in view. On the Jewish calendar, this would have been the fourteenth. Also, on the importance of this month being mentioned, Dr. McClain further points out that "for those who believe in Biblical inspiration and the genuineness of predictive prophecy, it will be no surprise to learn that the date fixed by Nehemiah happens to be one of the best known dates in ancient history. Even the Encyclopedia Britannica, certainly not biased in favor of prophecy, sets that date of Artaxerxes's accession as 465 BC; and therefore his twentieth year would be 445 BC. The month was Nissan, and since no day is given, according to Jewish Custom the date would be understood as the first. So in our calendar the date would be March 14, 445 BC. Here we have the beginning of the Seventy Weeks" (Dr. Alva J. McClain, *Daniel's Prophecy of the 70 Weeks*, Zondervan Publishing House, p. 24).

Having stated those facts about the sixty-nine weeks (483, or 69 x 7, Jewish years), it becomes obvious that before starting any calculation, we must first convert the 483 years into days (Illustration 2).

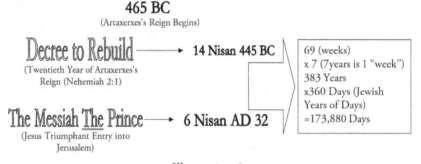

465 BC
(Artaxerxes's Reign Begins)

Decree to Rebuild ——→ **14 Nisan 445 BC**
(Twentieth Year of Artaxerxes's
Reign (Nehemiah 2:1)

The Messiah The Prince ——→ **6 Nisan AD 32**
(Jesus Triumphant Entry into
Jerusalem)

69 (weeks)
x 7 (7 years is 1 "week")
383 Years
x360 Days (Jewish
Years of Days)
=173,880 Days

Illustration 2

Once we do this, we can convert them into our years. Again, as a reminder, we're trying to prove whether the sixty-nine weeks or the total days of 173,880 can be verified as the time frame between the second decree of Artaxerxes and what we now know as "Palm Sunday." Dr. MacArthur summarizes this calculation from Anderson's book as follows (see also Illustration 3):

Working from March 14, 445 B.C. (the date of Artaxerxes' second decree), Sir Robert Anderson calculated by astronomical calendars and charts that the day of the Messiah's coming was April 6, A.D. 32. Such calendars and charts helped him find out the timing of the Jewish new moons by which the Passover were determined. One of the problems Anderson had to resolve in his calculations was that between the decree of Artaxerxes and the triumphant entry of Jesus into Jerusalem there appeared to be a period of 477 years and 24 days, not 483 years (sixty-nine prophetic weeks). After deducting one year to account for the fact that 1 B.C. and 1 A.D. are not two years but one, that left Anderson with a total of 476 years and 24 days or a total of 173,880 days. Anderson next added 119 days to his figure for the 119 leap years represented by 476 years. That results in a figure of 173,883 days—three days too many! But realizing that the Julian calendar on which our365-day year exceeds a solar year by $1/128^{th}$ of a day. That fraction of 476 years is three days, which when subtracted from 173,883 yields a difference of 173,880 days—precisely the number of days predicted in Daniel 9:25![1]

[1] John MacArthur, *John MacArthur's Bible Studies The Future of Israel: Daniel 9:20–12:13* (Chicago: Moody Press). Used with permission.

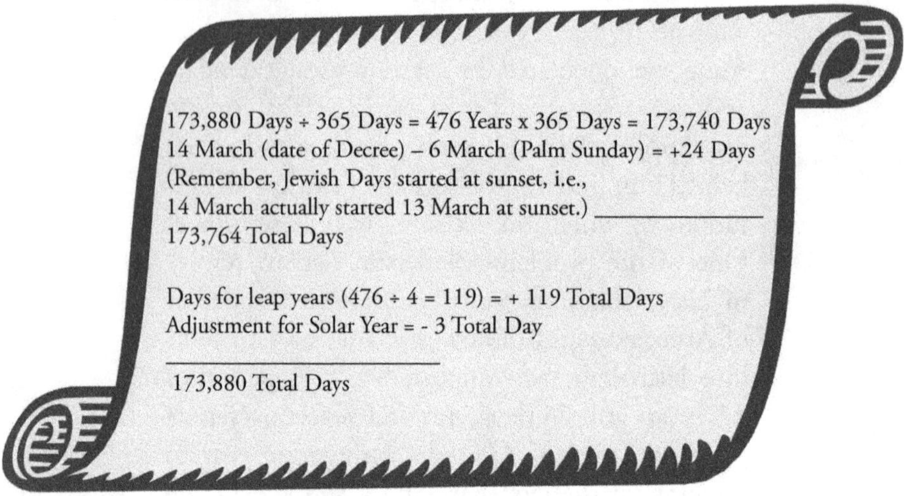

173,880 Days ÷ 365 Days = 476 Years x 365 Days = 173,740 Days
14 March (date of Decree) – 6 March (Palm Sunday) = +24 Days
(Remember, Jewish Days started at sunset, i.e.,
14 March actually started 13 March at sunset.) _____
173,764 Total Days

Days for leap years (476 ÷ 4 = 119) = + 119 Total Days
Adjustment for Solar Year = - 3 Total Day

_____
173,880 Total Days

Illustration 3

These facts clearly point out the preciseness and certainty of God's Word.

Having looked at the first part of this prophecy and its fulfillment, we are still left with one remaining week—the seventieth. Based on verse 25 and the first portion of verse twenty-six, it becomes obvious the sixty-ninth week ends with Jesus being proclaimed as Messiah. It is also obvious from the construction of the verses, there is a gap between week 69 and 70. This conclusion is based on the fact that up to the point of week 69, the angel had not only been giving Daniel specific events, but when they would start and end. However, when he comes to the end of the sixty-ninth week, he began to talk about events without any reference to time. These events are recorded in the latter portion of verse twenty-six of the ninth chapter of Daniel. It includes the fact that not only would their (the Jews) beloved temple be destroyed, but they would also cease to exist as a nation. Also, the trouble that would characterize their existence from then on (after the sixty-ninth week) would be similar to a flood. Although the angel does not tell Daniel how long his people will be in this predicament, he does let him know the event that will begin it. It would start when the "people of the prince who is to come shall destroy the city and the temple."

In understanding this phrase, two facts are seen that helps us. First, whatever event the angel has reference to, has to take place after the crucifixion.[1] Second, according to verse twenty-seven, these are part (the crucifixion being the other) of the events that separates week 69 from week 70. We know this because the seventieth week began as the first week, not with a decree but a covenant made between Israel ("the many") and an unidentified leader, whose identity (though not clearly given in that verse) is the Antichrist. There is disagreement among some theologians about "the many" in verse twenty-seven of the ninth chapter of Daniel. However, I believe if we allow Scripture to interpret Scripture, we will have little problem in identifying them as Israel; since the angel has already told Daniel the prophecy concerns "his people." Whenever another group or nation is intended, they are clearly identified as in the latter portion of verse twenty-six.

Having established these facts, let us now look at the events themselves. It is obvious the people in mind here are the Romans; in particular, Titus and his army during the seizure of Jerusalem in AD 67–70. Since this has been covered in a previous chapter, I see no need of repeating it here. However, what does need to be pointed out is the endless persecution and struggle the Jews are destined to go through. Based on this and other passages, especially those of Revelation twelve, this will characterize their plight in history all the way up through the middle of the tribulation period (Revelation 12:7–11; cf. Daniel 12:1).

The struggle and plight of the Jews will not be the only event that will characterize the gap between week 69 and 70. Other events will also occur as God's plan for man, Satan, and the world unfold. Some of these are the gathering of the nation of Israel out of the nations in the world to their own homeland (cf. Ezekiel 37:20–22),

---

[1] The reason for omitting the resurrection here is due to it not being mentioned in the prophecy. However, we do know that it is to be included as part of the events that separated week 69 from week 70.

and the reunification of the last empire in the form of a ten-toe or ten-horn confederacy (Daniel 2, 9). Added to this will be an apparent war involving Israel and the countries now occupying the land previously known as the Soviet Union (Ezekiel 38–39).

It is difficult to determine whether this battle recorded in Ezekiel occurs before the Seventieth Week or during this period. One thing that support its happening before is the fact that it will take seven years to burn the enemy's weapons (Ezekiel 39:9). If this happened during the last week, it would seem to contradict the peaceful entrance of Antichrist recorded in the second verse of the sixth chapter of Revelation. The other problem with this conclusion is the seeming war between the Antichrist and Israel recorded in Revelation twelve and her subsequent rescue and deliverance by God (cf. Revelation 12:13–16). The only certainty that we have of this event is that it will take place.

Another and perhaps most important reason for the gap between the sixty-ninth and seventieth week is the birth of the church. Before God created the world, He already determined that He would save a select group of people, whether Jew or Gentile, slave or free, rich or poor. They all would share in this blessing.

The Apostle Paul points out in the first chapter of his letter to the Ephesians that before the foundation of the world, God chose some to be saved (Ephesians 1:4). Although this mystery had not been reveal to us until the New Testament, it still does not deny the fact that this has always been His purpose. Without the life, death, and resurrection of Jesus Christ, this plan could not have been fulfilled. Until this point, it was not possible for man to be forgiven of his sins and enjoy the benefits that only salvation brings. He remained hostile to God, separated from Him, as Paul pointed out in the second chapter of Ephesians, without hope in this world or the world to come. Therefore, the most important purpose of this gap is that it was necessary so God could call out, from all nations, tribes, and tongues, His Elect people. This does not mean that God's elect only lived during this gap. Such a conclusion would deny the salvation of everyone in the Old Testament. The purpose of this gap was to secure their salvation as well. Until then, they were already just as justified as New Testament Christians. This is clearly the case, otherwise the Spirit would not have recorded that our justification is based on the same faith as Abraham (Romans 4:3, 16).

The Hebrew writer confirmed this further in his account of the faithful servants of God in the eleventh chapter of Hebrews (Hebrews 11:39). This list was only a small sample for which the writer himself point out that time would not allow him to list all the names of those who were justified by faith. However, before the crucifixion, they remained in Abraham's bosom until the works of the Son of God had accomplished their redemption. This is one point that seems to be ignored by those who would separate Old Testament saints from New Testament saints. This is a grave mistake; because what it says is the church is not one body, but two—one in the Old and one in the New—something that is unsupported by Scripture. Therefore, it is doing this gap that God is calling out from the world His elect people whom He chose from the foundation of the world (Illustration 4).

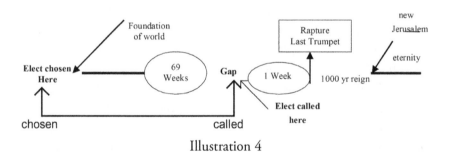

Illustration 4

Just as He allowed the people of Noah's day 120 years of grace before judging the world that first time, He has now paused the clock for a time known only to Him, the Son, and Holy Spirit. He will not only call out a people to Himself, but He will also use these same people as the means of proclaiming His marvelous Gospel to a lost world. Paul refers to this period of time as the age of the Gentiles (Romans 11:25). In using this term, he was not implying that God was finished with the nation Israel. He as much says so in his statement the Jews hardness will last only until "the fullness of the Gentiles has come in" (Romans 11:25, ESV). In this discourse, Paul is addressing the spiritual blindness of the Jews as well as the necessity of it. This was necessary so God could fulfill his purpose of engrafting the wild olive branches (Gentiles) into the good olive tree (Jews). The Jews have always been the people of promise, and therefore, salvation was extended to them first. This was not the case with the Gentiles. We were, as Paul tells the Ephesians, aliens and strangers from the commonwealth of Israel. However, during this gap, the wall that previously separated Jew from Gentile has been torn down by the atoning work of Christ. The result is a mystical union, which has united both Jew and Gentile into one body, united in the one purpose of glorifying God on earth (cf. Ephesians 2:13). This new body, or rather, new creation, has become the true Israel, God's holy nation and royal priesthood (cf. Romans 3:28; 1 Peter 2:9). The gap will then close once all of its citizens have been gathered in. As in the days of Noah, when the flood came, there was left no further opportunity for the lost to enter the ark of safety. While there are those who would dispute this fact, the book of Revelation is clear about this. At the end of the seal, trumpet, and bowl judgment, John records that despite all that had happened, men still refused to repent of their evil deeds and turn to God (cf. Revelation 9:20–21; 16:21).

It is interesting that one of the signs that would mark the closeness of Christ's return will be that the times would be like "the days of Noah" (Matthew 24:37). People would be marrying and giving in marriage, eating and drinking. What is meant by this phrase is the people in Noah's day did not see the urgency of the situation, nor the need to heed his warnings. Therefore, they went on about their daily activities as if though there was nothing wrong. This is the emphasis behind the description of the lifestyles of those living during the time of Noah. They were doing things common to everyday life.

A careful examination of the book of Genesis reveals another telling thing about the people's behavior that comes dangerously close to our day. They were not only carrying on with their everyday activities, but when God looked upon the earth; he saw "that the wickedness of man was great on the earth, and that every intent of the thoughts of his heart was only evil continually" (Genesis 6:5, 11

KJV). Since this time in history, the wickedness of man continues to increase; yet God still sends His messengers to warn the people. His grace continues to allow the sun to shine on the just and the unjust and the rain to water the earth that it may produce its fruit in due season. Soon, however, His justice and wrath will be poured out against man's sinfulness.

CHAPTER 12

THE SOUNDING OF THE LAST TRUMPET

In a moment, in the twinkling of an eye, at the last
trump: for the trumpet shall sound, and the dead shall
be raised incorruptible, and we shall be changed.
—1 Corinthians 15:52

In the previous chapters, I have tried to present scriptural evidence that point to certain events that must happen before Jesus Christ returns. In the remaining chapters, I hope to build on that foundation and give further evidence that suggest Christ's return will not occur before the end of the Seventieth Week of Daniel.

From the first time I heard about the Rapture and the return of Christ, I held and strongly defended the pretribulation view (that Christ comes before the tribulation) of this doctrine. However, an article published by the Worldwide Church of God in the late eighties challenged my belief. The article presented a compelling argument about events surrounding the last trumpet. Although I did not support them doctrinally in this area, I did find that it raised questions that had never occurred to me. Up to that point, I had heard nothing but a pretribulation view of the Rapture, so this was a whole new world to me. Although I had no idea the Worldwide Church of God was not part of mainstream Christianity (then), my desire for knowledge drove me to their teachings as well as to the

Jehovah's Witnesses and Mormons (not necessarily about eschatology). However, I thank God, that through his Spirit, he exposed me to the errors of the Worldwide Church as well as other cults through the writings of the late Dr. Walter Martin. Through his tape ministry and the exhaustive research presented in his book, *The Kingdom of the Cults,* I was delivered from the devil's deception and brought into a deeper and clearer understanding of the Word of God. More importantly, I learned the need of studying the Holy Scripture for oneself and sifting all other teachings through its truths.

When one fails to use the Bible as the final arbiter for all that is heard or read, we become easy prey to false teachers. Their messages, which appeal to the flesh, can easily lead one astray. The reason for this is that a person's environment, tradition, and own biases heavily influence their beliefs (Illustration 1).

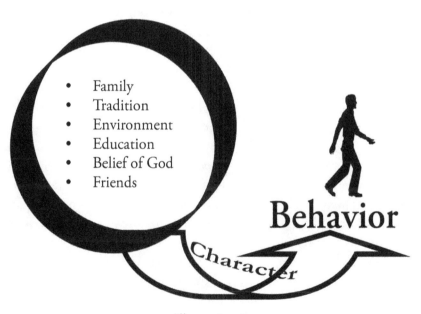

- Family
- Tradition
- Environment
- Education
- Belief of God
- Friends

Behavior

Character

Illustration 1

False teachers understand this and tailor their messages accordingly. This explains the widespread success of televangelists (not all) who have successfully convinced many Christians that God's will for their lives is wealth, prosperity, and freedom from sickness and diseases. If the teachers who spout such errors put their teachings under the microscope of Scripture, their membership would decrease drastically.

A person's willingness to yield to the Holy Spirit's power and influence and meditating on God's word determines the degree of their spiritual strength and maturity. Scripture supports the truth that it is not possible to fully yield to the Spirit without a thorough knowledge of God's word. This is the reason that doctrine is so important to the Church. When instructing young Titus, Paul emphasized the importance of holding fast to sound doctrine (teaching). As long as he did so, he would be able by "sound doctrine both to exhort and to convince the gainsayers" (Titus 1:9). Only sound or healthy doctrine can build the Body of Christ into the people we need to be. It should govern and control every aspect of our life. According to the Psalmist, it is a lamp unto our feet, lighting up our pathway and pointing out dangers that lurk in the darkness. During these last days when there are so many false teachers both in and out of the church, Christians need to have God's pure word more than ever, especially about the last days or eschatology.

Through the power of the Holy Spirit, this writer's zeal and passion for this particular doctrine has been unyielding, and like Jeremiah, I couldn't contain it even if I wanted to throughout the years, no matter how much I have studied, there always remained this question about the last trumpet. Why is it mentioned in both New Testament passages (1 Corinthians 15:51–52; 1 Thessalonians 4:13–18) that deal with the Rapture? The answers given by most pretribulation teachers did not satisfy me but instead raised the kind of questions mentioned earlier. It was such restlessness in my soul and a sincere need to know God's word in this area that eventually exposed me to the article mentioned earlier. As I look back on those days to where God has brought me now, I clearly see His providential hand in all that has happened.

So what about this question of the last trumpet? Paul closes his second letter to the Christians at Corinth (1 Corinthian 15) by highlighting the importance of the resurrection of Christ and its relationship to our resurrection and the Rapture (1 Corinthians 15:1–12). He points out that if there is no future resurrection of the dead, Christ was not resurrected. Furthermore, our preaching is in vain and so is our faith if we preach Christ's resurrection and it's not true. We have become, in the truest sense, false witnesses against God, claiming that he raised Jesus from the dead when He did not. Furthermore, he continues, if there was no resurrection, we are still in our sins, still under its bondage and ultimately under the wrath and condemnation of God. As if that's not bad enough, he drives home the point by declaring, if this is the message taught, believed and preached by Christians universally, we are to be pitied above all men; because the very foundation of the message we preach, the message that so many men and women have and continue to die for is the biggest hoax in history (1 Corinthians 15:13–20).

However, thank God this was and is not the case! Christ did indeed rise from the dead, and because He rose, we know that one day we will also rise. To further strengthen the Christians at Corinth in this glorious doctrine, Paul explains the nature of the resurrected body. It's sown or buried corrupt, but is raised incorruptible, immortal, and no longer subject to the physical laws of nature (1 Corinthians 15:35–50).

But it is in the latter portion of that same chapter where he addresses the question of the last trumpet (vv. 52–58). In this regard, Paul points out that "Behold, I tell you a mystery; we shall not all sleep, but we shall be changed, In a moment, in the twinkling of an eye, at the last trumpet; for the trumpet will sound, and the dead will be raised imperishable, and we shall be changed" (vv. 51–52 KJV).

First, Paul lets us know that what he is about to tell us is a mystery. Normally, when we speak of this word, we have in mind something that is obscure or beyond our ability to grasp. Although it does carry this meaning in some portions of Scripture, such as when Paul speaks of the world inability to understand Christ's identity and by it crucified Him (1 Corinthians 2:7; cf. 2 Thessalonians 2:7; 1 Timothy 3:16), he also uses it in this sense when he speaks about the "mystery of lawlessness" in the second chapter of Second Thessalonians. Its most common use in the New Testament, especially in the Pauline writings, is about truths previously hidden, but is now revealed. For example, in Paul's letter to the Ephesians, he mention the mystery "of Christ, which in other ages were not made known unto the sons of men, as it is now revealed unto His holy apostles and prophets by the Spirit" (Ephesians 2:5,6 KJV). He explains the truth of "the Gentiles" being "fellow heirs, and of the same body, and partakers of his promise in Christ by the Gospel" was hidden until the New Testament was written. Before this revelation was made known through the Apostle Paul, the idea of Gentiles being able to receive all the rights and privileges reserved for the Jews was inconceivable. But now, says Paul, God has revealed this truth through the Gospel (cf. Ephesians 2:13–18). It is no longer a mystery. Plainly put then, the term *mystery* in the New Testament has to do with the truths of God. Truths that have always been there but were incomprehensible to our natural senses—God the Holy Spirit must illumine our darkened mind to these truths!

This is how we are to understand its use in the fifteenth chapter of First Corinthians. Before Paul wrote this letter, the teaching of the resurrection was not a new teaching. Not only was it not new, it was believed and accepted as an actuality by most Jews (the Sadducees being the exception), as evident by Martha's comment to Jesus about Lazarus's resurrection (John 11:34). We also know the primary teaching that separated the Pharisees and Sadducees was the matter of whether there was going to be a resurrection (Acts 23:6–8). Both Old Testament writers, Job (19:26) and Daniel (12:2) spoke of a future resurrection. However, what was hidden from them was the fact there would be two separated by a literal thousand years (Revelation 20:4–6, 11–14). The first one consists of the resurrected, glorified bodies of the saints only, which will look the same on the outside but completely changed physiologically.

The second thing that he reveals is that the change will take place at the last trump or during the last trumpet. Throughout the Bible, trumpets played a major role in major events in Jewish society. For example, the year of Jubilee (Leviticus 25:9), assembling the people for battle (Numbers 10:1–9), as well as an instrument of praise unto the Lord (Psalm 150:3) were all celebrated or initiated by the blowing of a trumpet. These are but a few examples of how the nation of Israel used trumpets. However, the one that is of particular interest to our discussion is the trumpet sounded during the year of jubilee. The Hebrew word for jubilee means "a blast of the trumpet." During this time, the trumpets sounded throughout the land. Harvesting would stop to give the land its year of rest, slaves were freed, and all debts canceled.

When I look at the time leading up to the year of jubilee, I see a picture of the church age and the millennium. After the ascension of Christ, the world essentially began its seasons of harvest. For the time being, we're all enjoying a time of sowing and reaping. Some are sowing to destruction and eternal damnation, while others are sowing seeds of righteousness and will reap eternal rewards. But soon the sowing will end and the time of harvest will be upon the world. The trumpet will sound and the Lord will send His angels to gather His elect from the earth (Matthew 24:31). At this harvesting, the people of God will enter their day of rest and will begin to enjoy their eternal rewards (cf. Hebrews. 4:1–7). While it's true the unsaved who escape the wrath of God during the Great Tribulation will enter the Millennium Kingdom, their existence will still be incomparable to ours. According to Scripture they, along with all the unsaved who have died since the beginning of time, will face the righteous judge at the end of the millennium to receive judgment for deeds done during their lifetime (Revelation 20:11–15).

When studying passages on the end-times, it is always best, whenever possible, to try and find illustrations or examples from the Old Testament relating to it. However, in doing so, we must rely on the Spirit to avoid taking a few verses, especially those just mentioned, and try to build a whole doctrine or movement. If nothing else, I did learn one thing from my involvement with the Jehovah's Witnesses, and that is, one can easily take a couple of scriptures and build a very convincing lie. It does not matter whether it's done intentionally or unintentionally, the point is, it's still a lie, and if believed, will lead many astray. Therefore, to avoid this, I would like to compare this particular passage in first Corinthian with its parallel passage in the fourth chapter of the book of 1 Thessalonians. The value and necessity of allowing Scripture to interpret Scripture is brought out when we do not isolate these two passages but read them together. In doing so, we remain true to sound hermeneutical principles and avoid the potential and temptation to read between the lines and arrive at a wrong interpretation. The other reason for doing so is to clearly show that it is unlikely the resurrection of the saints can take place before the end of Daniel's Seventieth Week.

In these two letters, the Holy Spirit gives Paul a startling revelation of what will take place at the second coming. In his first letter to the Corinthians, he tells us that it will happen in the following sequence:

- We shall all be changed (1 Corinthians 15:51a).
- It will happen in the twinkling of an eye (1 Corinthians 15:52a).
- It will take place at the last trump (1 Corinthians 15:52b).

However, as was the case with Daniel (12:2) and Job (19:26), he apparently was given only a general revelation (or chose to omit it) about the resurrection, because he leaves out specific details in 1 Corinthians that are included in his letters to the Thessalonians. In other words, all he tells us in that passage (1 Corinthians) is the fact that it takes place at the last trumpet and that our bodies will be changed. He does not really address the question in regard to those of us who will be alive when Christ return. Without this crucial information, it would seem, or could be said by some, that those Christians who are alive at Christ's return will be left behind, or somehow excluded from participation in this event. However, what was left veiled and concealed to the Corinthians was later given to the church in his letters to the Thessalonians. As stated earlier, they thought that those who had already died would miss the Rapture and the return of Christ.

To add clarity to his teaching, Paul provided additional facts surrounding this event. In addition to what he had already written in regard to this matter, he calms the Thessalonians' fears by teaching them that the Second Coming and Rapture would occur in the following sequence:

- Christ will descend from heaven with those (their souls or spirits) who have died in him (1 Thessalonians 4:14,16).
- This will be accompanied with a shout, with the voice of the archangel, and with the trumpet of God (1 Thessalonians 4:16).
- The dead (physical bodies of Christians only) will rise (raptured) to be reunited with their spirit (soul) in the air (1 Thessalonians 4:16c).
- Those of us still alive (Christians only) will be caught (raptured) up to meet our Lord in the sky (1 Thessalonians 4:17).

When compared with our Lord's own words about this same time period in the twenty-forth chapter of Matthew, we find they are strikingly similar. Christ said that "He will send His angels with a great trumpet and they will gather His elect from the four winds, from one end of the sky to the other" (Matthew 24:31 KJV). What's interesting and of particular note in this passage, especially in light of 1 Corinthians 15:52, is that all this takes place after the Son of Man appears in the sky (v. 30). There is no reason that we should interpret the Lord's statement that these things will happen "immediately after the tribulation" as meaning anything other than just that. This statement by our Lord would seem to point to a post-Tribulation Rapture. The idea of all or a majority of those events mentioned in the Olivet Discourse applying only to Israel and not Christians is problematic to say the least. First, it says that the one place our Lord chose to speak so clearly about His second coming was given to those who rejected Him. Second, it says He directed His message to a people who are both spiritually blind and dead. If either of these statements are true, Paul could never have said of them they were "in Him."

In the letters to the seven churches, Christ closed them all with these words, "He that hath an ear, let him hear." He spoke as He did for a good reason. The Word goes out to all, both Jew and Gentile, believer and unbeliever alike. However, to the unsaved, it is foolishness. To them, it is utter nonsense, according to Paul (1 Corinthians 2:7–8, 14). To expect and believe that unbelieving Jews will understand and accept this portion of Scripture without being born again is truly a stretch. The only way that they can is to be regenerated. Then and only then will their blinded eyes be opened (cf. Matthew 13:10–15)! This is the only way they, as is the case with all Christians, will be able to see clearly what the Spirit is saying to the church.

The point of examining the passages in Matthew, First Corinthians and First Thessalonians was to point out the Second Coming takes place at the last trumpet. Having proved this fact, the only thing left is to find out which trumpet is in view and when is it blown. We will look at this in more detail in the chapters to come.

CHAPTER 13

THE LAST TRUMP AND THE LORD'S RETURN

And unto them were given seven trumpets.
—Revelation 8:2b

The only book in the New Testament, and in the whole Bible, that talks about trumpets sounding is Revelation. Therefore, to understand when the last trumpet will sound, a good understanding of the book's chronology is paramount. As it was necessary to do this when discussing the Antichrist's rise to power in chapter eight, so it becomes necessary to do so from the perspective of the seven trumpets. All attempts made in trying to understand the various visions, symbols, and numbers associated with it and the other six trumpets will be an effort laden with frustration and futility. This is not to say that much cannot be learned without this process. However, in order to fully appreciate and understand the last trumpet and all that happens when it's blown, we must put the book in some sort of logical order.

But, before we start this process, we need to examine the book's theme found in verse nineteen of chapter one. When we do so, we find the book of Revelation has three basic divisions (Illustration 1).

Illustration 1

Having established these divisions, the only thing left is to identify the point of reference. Failure to keep and read the book in these divisions will make it impossible to get a proper understanding of the overall theme and purpose of the book.

Nearly all commentators agree the most obvious point of reference for all three divisions is that of John's immediate circumstance. In other words, all the events centers around John's exile on the Island of Patmos. Therefore, Christ's appearance in chapter one represents those things happening in the past. By past, I mean the appearance of Christ in chapter one had already happened from the perspective of what John is doing from chapters two to the end of the book. In other words, Christ's appearance had already occurred, and John was now writing the letters to the seven churches as Christ had directed. Although these were seven literal churches that were in existence during his exile, they were not the only ones. Christ's selection of these particular seven was twofold. First, its immediate purpose was to address the state of these specific churches in Asia Minor. Second, it was for the benefit of all Christians in every age.

We first see these two truths in the number seven, which in numerology means perfection or completeness. Dr. John MacArthur points out that these churches represent Christ's total message to His total church throughout the Church Age. So when we look at them, we see the birth of the church in the letter to Ephesus and the waning of the church in the letter to the Laodicean church. A careful study of church history easily corroborates this. The church started out as a wildfire, turning the world upside down. Seeing them as a threat, the various Roman emperors, especially Diocletian[1], tried to destroy her through severe persecution. Church history aptly chronicles this period and supports the fact that the churches of Ephesus and Smyrna symbolically represented this period.

The severe persecution and bloodshed begun by the Roman Emperor Diocletian ended in AD 311 with the signing of an edict of toleration by Galerius, the Roman ruler of the eastern portion of the empire. The most interesting person on the world's stage after Diocletian and Galerius, as it relates to church history, was Constantine. His rise to the throne of Rome was due largely (in this writer's mind) to a dream. In this dream, he supposedly saw a blazon cross in the sky and heard a voice that said, "In this sign conquer.[1]" As a result, he and his army were able to defeat Rome's final stronghold and seize control over the city. There is no need to venture into a long-drawn-out discussion about whether he did or did not see a sign and what he heard, since it does not lend to our discussion. The only point in bringing it up at all is to highlight the result of what happened—mainly that, as a result, the course of church history changed drastically. No longer was Christ regarded as the only head of the visible church. The church now became united to the state (Rome), so being born in Rome meant that you were also born into the Church of Jesus Christ.

However, true Christians in Christ recognized no leader other than Christ and refused to give allegiance and homage to emperors and the church-state. As a result, they became enemies of the empire. The churches of Pergamum and Thyatira symbolized this marriage between the church and the state. Eventually, the power of the state and church gradually merged and became less and less discernable from each other. In the sixteenth century, God moved on the heart of a monk named Martin Luther and reversed this trend during the Protestant Reformation. This was another important landmark that, again, changed the course of church history. Although Martin Luther and others were able to restore the essential doctrines of the church,

---

[1] Bruce L. Shelley, *Church History in Plain Language*, Updated Second Edition (Thomas Nelson Inc., 1996).

they did not abandon all the things that Rome introduced into the church. Sardis represents this era. She had begun a good work but did not complete it.

The great revivals and the spread of the Gospel throughout the world came on the heels of the Reformation. The church of Philadelphia where Jesus opened a door that no one can shut symbolized this period. The same could be said of them as was said of the early church: they turned the world upside down. However, that era has given way to a period where the church has lost her zeal. She no longer has the zeal of the past, nor does it seem like her footing is solidly implanted in the doctrines of the Apostles and Prophets. The Laodicean church is characteristic and symbolic of all this. She is neither hot nor cold.

There are those who would insist that Laodicea has no reference to the real church at all, but instead is an apostate church that will exist during the Tribulation period. This poses a serious problem for those who believe and teach this because as stated earlier, nearly all theologians agree that seven in the book of Revelation represents completeness. To say that Laodicea is apostate not only put before us an incomplete church, but goes directly against Christ's own declaration at the beginning of the book that He stands "in the midst of the seven churches," not in the midst of the six churches. It is inconceivable to this writer that Jesus would include an apostate church as part of what is regarded as a unique group.

The relevance of this is crucial when it comes to the Second Coming because, as pointed out from a previous chapter, there exists a gap between the sixty-ninth and seventieth week. It is during this gap that God is calling out from the nations His elect people, the church. I believe that "gap" is also the period which comprise all of chapters two and three of Revelation. During this time frame, God is not only dealing with His physical nation (gathering them back to their homeland) and the Gentiles, but His spiritual nation (the church) as well. On the one hand, God is preparing the world for the appearing of Antichrist while on the other He is creating a new Israel from the spiritual seed of Abraham-Jesus Christ (Galatians 3:29). This writer believes strongly the Laodicean period ends with the salvation of the last person. When that happens, the "gap" closes and ushers in the fourth and fifth chapters of Revelation. I do not make such a radical statement without support. Therefore, I direct the reader's attention to the ninth chapter of Revelation where we read these words, "And the rest of people, the ones not killed by these plagues, did not repent from the works of their hands, so that they should not worship devils, and idols of gold, and silver, and brass, and stone, and of wood: which neither can see nor hear, nor walk" (Revelation 9:20–21 KJV). This verse obviously has in mind all the plagues included in the seven seals, and sixth of the seven trumpets. The importance of these verses is the fact they summarize man's response after God's judgment of all the plagues which comprise the seventh trumpet and the end of the Seventieth Week or the Great Tribulation, as well as the Beast's reign (Revelation 13:5; cf. Revelation 11:3, 7, 11–15; 12:13). This passage and Romans 11:25 clearly explain there will not be a great revival during the Tribulation period. The saints martyred during that period are those who are alive during that time.

So what does all this have to do with the seventh trumpet and the Rapture? As stated earlier, the common belief about the Rapture is that it occurs before the Tribulation period; while "Post-Tribulationists" believe that it occurs after this period. One of the key verses used by most Pre-Tribulationists is Revelation 4:1. In that passage, the Lord's commands John to "come up hither." Most, if not all, Pre-Tribulationists teach that in that command, John represents the church, and the voice that sounded like the trumpet refers to the last trumpet.

Although this does sound logical and seemingly would support a Pre-Tribulation Rapture, it does not fit the overall structure of the book. The first problem presented by this teaching is that throughout the book, John is taken back and forth between heaven and earth. For example, in chapter four, he is in heaven, but in chapter seven, he's plainly back on earth again according to verse one. These transitions occur continuously throughout the book since sometimes an act is carried out in heaven, but its actions are carried out on earth. Are we to gather from this the church goes up and down from Heaven as well?

The other justification for a pre-Tribulation Rapture is based on the idea that since the church is not mentioned after chapter four, it obviously means that it must have been removed from the world. However, such a conclusion is unfounded because the command is not directed to the church, but to John. As a matter of fact, the church is nowhere mentioned in verse one of chapter four either implicitly or explicitly. The command is directed specifically to John for the express purpose of showing him those "things which must be hereafter." He is the only one raptured (in a sense) at this point in a manner unexplained and uncharacteristic of the rapture of the church (cf. 1 Corinthians 15:50–52; 1 Thessalonians 4:13–17). The only interpretation of what happened to John in chapter four is that he is in the spirit in the complete sense of the word (cf. 2 Corinthians 12:2). It is difficult for us to understand to what extent his experience was. Some go so far as to compare it to an out-of-body experience. I'm not willing to go that far, but I will agree that it was something similar or close to it. Dr. Kenneth Wuest offers this explanation, that it is being "so absolutely controlled by the Holy Spirit, that their physical senses of sight, hearing, feeling, were not registered so far as any recognized impressions were concerned. It was as if they were temporarily outside of their bodies. The control of the Holy Spirit over their faculties was such that He could give them the visions" (Kenneth S. Wuest, *Word Studies in the Greek New Testament, Volume III,* Eerdmans Publishing Company).

In either case, we do know that John (unlike Paul who was also given glimpses of heaven and forbidden to speak about what he saw) was taken to heaven and told to "write down" all that he saw.

What John records in chapters four and five is the most magnificent and glorious scene of heaven ever depicted in the Bible. Even as I try to write about it, I'm overwhelmed by how beautiful and wonderful a place heaven must be. Even in his heightened state of spirituality, John at times could hardly find words to explain what he saw. A throne was set or placed in heaven and on that throne was seemingly the eternal God. This within itself is amazing and incomprehensible, since God is spirit and omnipresent. We're not told how this was possible, but by faith, we understand that all things are possible with God. In either case, as John continues to describe this heavenly court scene, a scroll held in the right hand of God draws his attention. A call goes out to every living creature in existence to find one worthy enough to remove the seals on the scroll to reveal its contents. The fact of John's weeping coupled with the fact that no one was found worthy enough to open the scroll highlights its importance. It is obvious the scroll contained everything written from the sixth chapter of Revelation to the end of the book. As long as the scroll remained sealed, its message remained hidden from us. As Christ takes the book from His Father's hand, there is an outburst of praise from the Heavenly Host showing the Lamb's worthiness to take the scroll and remove its seal. From that point in time, the gap that began at the close of the sixty-ninth week of Daniel begins to slowly close. It does not fully close since the restrainer has not removed his hand from the man of sin: the Antichrist.

CHAPTER 14

THE SEVEN SEALS OF REVELATION

And I saw in the right hand of him that sat on the throne a book
written within and on the backside, sealed with seven seals.
—Revelation 5:1

Having concluded the Seventieth Week began with the opening of the sixth seal along with the fact that the thirteenth and seventeenth chapters of Revelation tells us how the Antichrist rises to
power, we can now find out when the seventh trumpet sounds. To do
this, I again point out the logical sequence of the book of Revelation.
In explaining the relationship that exist between the seals, trumpets,
and bowls, Dr. Macarthur uses the example of a telescope (Illustration
1).

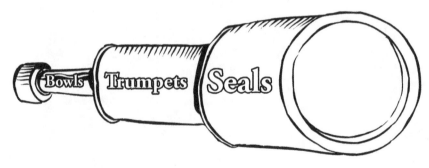

Illustration 1

In using this illustration, he provides a vivid picture of how everything that happens in Revelation unfolds from the seventh seal. That is, all the trumpet judgments, and all the bowl judgments unfold from the seventh seal the same way as the various sections of a telescope does.[1] When we view the overall book of Revelation from this perspective, it becomes clear the seventh trumpet cannot sound before removal of the last seal. Another important point that must be stressed is the manner in which these scrolls were sealed. The seals were not all affixed to the front of it as if only to secure it from unrolling; instead, they were applied to its edges to conceal specific portions of its contents. It was for this reason that during the time of John, all wills and deeds of property were sealed by the owner and could only be opened by his legal representative.[2] They were rolled in a manner where one portion was rolled and a seal affixed to the edge and then another portion rolled and sealed. This process was repeated until the whole roll was sealed. With the one John saw, it had been rolled and sealed with seven seals. As each seal is removed, only those things and events that comprised that portion of the scroll were revealed.[3] For example, when the first seal was removed, John only saw the rider on the white horse because that was all that was contained in that part of the scroll. When the seventh seal is removed, the entire scroll is opened, and everything that remained in that portion began to unfold: the seven trumpets, the seven bowls, and all the plagues associated with them.

When we get to the seventh seal, we find an interesting thing occurring before its removal. God pauses everything for His servants to be sealed on their forehead. The identity of these servants will be addressed later in the book; suffice it to say here that they are God's people. The reasoning for their being sealed at this point is to protect them against the upcoming plagues.

After sealing the 144,000 servants, silence replaced the praise and worship in heaven for "half an hour," according to verse one of chapter eight. After this silence is over, we're given a picture of an

---

[1]   Dr. John MacArthur's Audio Tape Series on Revelation, 1970

[2]

[3]   *Ibid.*

angel whose responsibility it was to offer much incense "with the prayers of all saints on the golden altar which was before the throne." After which, the smoke of the incense "which came with the prayers of the saints, ascended up before God out of the angel's hand. And the angel took the censer, and filled it with fire off the altar, and cast it into the earth: and there were voices, and thunderings, and lightnings, and an earthquake" (Revelation 8:3–5). This awesome scene, now being witnessed by John must have been overwhelming! To be granted the blessing and privilege of beholding such an amazing act makes one understand why Paul was given a thorn in the flesh when he "heard unspeakable words, which it is not lawful for a man to utter" (2 Corinthians 12:4). However, what is even more amazing than this scene are the ones following the blowing of the six trumpets covered in the rest of chapters eight and nine. If we thought the world was in a mess and the hearts of men trembled from the results of the six seals, it is even more so after these trumpets are blown. One third of the trees will be burned up, one third of the sea will be turned into blood, one third of the world's water supply will become contaminated, daylight will be shortened, and one third of all people (don't forget, the previous plagues killed 25 percent of the world's population) will be killed.

Seeing all these things happening around them and seemingly knowing that it is from God (cf. Revelation 6:16–17) still does not move unbelievers to repent of their sins and turn to the living God. Instead, they do what man always does when it comes to recognizing God and their sinfulness before Him—blaspheme His name even more. What this clearly proves is that, if God does not directly move on man's hardened and rebellious heart, he will never on his own admit his need for His love, grace, and mercy. Besides Romans chapter three, there is perhaps no greater picture in the New Testament that speaks to this fact. It is man's total inability in choosing God that makes salvation unattainable apart from the redemptive work of God the Son and the regenerative power of God the Spirit. Ultimately, this is the reason that man will still turn their backs on God, even under such terrible conditions as revealed during the plagues of the seals, trumpets, and bowls.

CHAPTER 15

THE END

And I saw, and behold a white horse: and
he that sat on him had a bow.

—Revelation 6:2

The purpose of the previous chapters was to lay before the reader, in chronological order, the events that will characterize the last seven years of the world. This had to be done to get an accurate picture, not necessarily of when the seventh trumpet sounds, but when the Lord will return. Since this is the author's major theme, failure to address the particular concern put forth by the disciples in the twenty-fourth chapter of Matthew defeats the purpose of the book.

Before we can end our discussion on the last trumpet, we must first look at chapter ten and the first portion of chapter eleven of the book of Revelation. The reasoning for this is that both chapters are a prelude to this event and provide invaluable information about what is happening. In general, chapter ten seems to stress that when the seventh trumpet sounds, "the mystery of God should be finished, as he hath declared to his servants the prophets" (Revelation 10:7). This statement probably means God is finally wrapping up His revelation about the end of the world, and the fate of man. The prophets had spoken of this time, especially Daniel, but neither they nor their contemporaries understood what it all meant. When the seventh trumpet sounds, God will uncover and fulfilled the full meaning of those prophetic sayings and visions.

Also in chapter ten is the issue of this mighty angel's identity. Theologians continue their debate on this angel's identity with little or no consensus. Many believe, based on his description alone, he has to be Christ. However, I believe certain statements made by him, such as the oath in verse ten, and the fact, he is said to be an angel, makes it difficult to accept or believe that he is Christ. The fact John identifies him as a mighty angel does not prove it, since this is not a title ever given to Jesus Christ. In the Old Testament for example, whenever He appeared in His preincarnate state, His title was "The Angel of the Lord" and never just as an "angel" or as simply "an angel of the Lord."

Since the book of Revelation is deeply grounded in Old Testament terminology and truths, it would not make sense for the Spirit to use a term for Christ that was different from that used in the Old Testament. While this would have been a nonissue for a Gentile, it would not have been so of the Apostle John. This is especially true when we understand that his only knowledge of angels would have been based on the writings and teachings of the Old Testament, since the canonization of the New Testament had not yet occurred. Let me emphasize here, I'm not saying that John was unfamiliar with the reality of angels; but instead, that he would have understood the difference between the terms *a mighty angel* and *the Angel of the Lord*. Granted, the appearance of this angel would seem to be Christ, especially because of the graphic picture depicted of him straddling land and sea. The only other reference of such an occurrence is that of the Angel of the Lord (which I take to be a Christophany or Jesus Christ) recorded in the first book of the Old Testament book of Chronicles (1 Chronicles 21:16). But again, this should not surprise us, since we are talking about a mighty angel who performs an act no more incredible than that performed by the angel in the fifth chapter of Revelation. That angel's voice was powerful enough for every living creature, both in heaven, earth and in Hell to hear it.

Added to the description of the angel in Revelation chapter ten is he swears "by him that liveth for ever and ever, who created heaven, and the things that therein are, and the earth, and the things that therein are, and the sea, and the things which are therein" (v. 6, KJV). This is almost a direct quote from Colossians chapter one (vv. 16–17) of Christ as Creator. By making such an oath, this angel is obviously swearing on behalf of someone much greater than himself. Since all three Persons within the Godhead are coequal in authority, I cannot see how this could be Christ. Granted, that as the Son of God He willingly subordinated Himself (functionally) to the Father; but that would not apply here since this being's title is simply a "mighty angel."

The other relevant fact presented in the tenth chapter is the sounding of the seventh trumpet suggests the end of time. Questions remain about what is being alluded to by the phrase *time will be no more.* Does he have in mind the mystery of God's plan or the culmination of God's judgment? Based on what is to happen next as part of the bowl judgments, I believe the latter explanation is in view. In a sense, the angel is saying that man's time is up, and God's judgment is imminent. I also believe that it is at this point the seven years ends or is ending because of the statement in Revelation chapter eleven (v. 7) about the two witnesses being killed (Illustration 1). Since their commission was only for three and a half years, their death signals the end of their ministry, and therefore, so must the seven years.

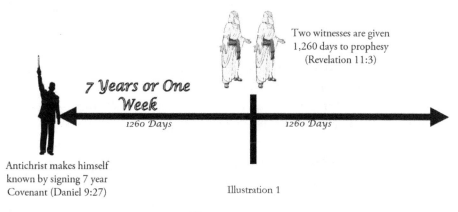

Two witnesses are given 1,260 days to prophesy (Revelation 11:3)

7 Years or One Week

1260 Days   1260 Days

Antichrist makes himself known by signing 7 year Covenant (Daniel 9:27)

Illustration 1

Illustration 1

From verses eight through fourteen of chapter eleven, we not only see the jubilee displayed by the world at the death of these two men, but more importantly, their resurrection at the end of three days. It is in verse fifteen of chapter eleven where the seventh trumpet sounds, and I believe, is also the point where the Rapture of the saints and the events recorded in the first fourteenth verses of chapter nineteen occurs.

After the seventh trumpet blows, there remains only seventy-five days left before the world ends (Daniel 12:11, 12 cf. Revelation 11:11, 15). This essential piece of information is only found in the twelfth chapter of the book of Daniel where the angel tells Daniel: "And from the time that the daily sacrifice shall be taken away, and the abomination that maketh desolate set up, there shall be a thousand two hundred and ninety days. Blessed is he that waiteth, and cometh to the thousand three hundred and five and thirty days" (Daniel 12:11–12 KJV). When these days are looked at with the seventieth week of Daniel, we find that it exceeds that time by seventy-five days.

To understand how we arrive at these extra days, we need to look at the third verse of the eleventh chapter of the book of Revelation where the angel tells John (on behalf of God) "I will give power unto my two witnesses, and they shall prophesy a thousand two hundred and threescore days, clothed in sackcloth" (KJV). Although this verse has as its focus God's two witnesses, it is also a reference point for the verses cited from the twelfth chapter of Daniel. The following passages must also be examined to complete the picture.

> When ye therefore shall see the abomination of desolation, spoken of by Daniel the prophet, stand in the holy place, (whoso readeth, let him understand). (Matthew 24:15 KJV)

> Who opposeth and exalteth himself above all that is called God, or that is worshipped; so that he as God sitteth in the temple of God, shewing himself that he is God. (2 Thessalonians 2:4 KJV)

Having identified all the proper passages of Scriptures regarding the seventy-five days, let us now begin to see how they all fit together. First, there is the Daniel passage, where we're told in verse eleven the total number of days from the period of time when the Antichrist stops the daily sacrifice is 1,290. We must find out two things before we can begin to understand what's happening in this verse. First, what time frame is in view and what sacrifice is the angel referring? The answer to the first question is the angel has to have the last days in view because of what was said in the first two verses of chapter twelve. The events spoken of there, especially in verse two, can only apply to the last days. In other words, the angel tells Daniel about a resurrection that will involve both the just and unjust. Based on the book of Revelation, we know the angel had two separate resurrections in view (Revelation 20:4–6; 11–15).

But what of the second question? It becomes obvious that if the time frame in view is the last days, then the sacrifice spoken of by the angel must also have the last days in mind. The single act that will identify "the Antichrist" is the signing of a seven-year covenant. Based on verse eleven of the twelfth chapter of Daniel, part of this agreement will be the construction of the Temple and the implementation of the daily sacrifices. The reasoning for this conclusion is based on the Lord's own word in the fifteenth verse of the twenty-forth chapter of Matthew. In that passage, He tells us that a person will desecrate (abomination of desolation) the temple by standing in the holy place. Many theologians would like to assign this prophecy to the actions of Antiochus Epiphanes, who, in 168 BC, erected a pagan altar in the temple. The only problem with such an interpretation is that Jesus could not have had a past event in mind because in verse twenty-one of Matthew twenty-four, He speaks of a time the world has never known before. Added to that is verse twenty-two of that same chapter where He speaks of shortening the days because of the elect's sake. Besides, what would be the point in telling His disciples to watch for an event that had already happened?

To clear up this matter, Paul identifies this man as being the Antichrist in his second letter to the church at Thessalonica. Therefore, based on what has been said, we can infer the Jews will rebuild their Temple sometime during the Tribulation Period. Second, the Jews will reinstitute the daily sacrifice, and lastly, at some point during the Tribulation Period, the Antichrist will desecrate the Temple by seating himself in the Holy of Holies (Matthew 24:15, 2 Thessalonians 2:4).

All that has been said so far was necessary to provide the background that helps us in our understanding of where the seventy-five days come from. As stated earlier, when the Antichrist's appears on the world scene, the last week of Daniel's Seventy Weeks begins. Besides this information, we are told he will break the covenant in the middle of the week. From this, I gather that one of the things that will characterize this action will be him sitting in the temple and declaring himself to be God (2 Thessalonians 2:4). This is the point in time the 1,290 days must be calculated from because it not only identifies the "abomination of desolation" but also the end of the daily sacrifice.

This conclusion is based on the events recorded in the twelfth chapter of Revelation where we find recorded two separate spiritual battles between Michael and Satan. We must view these two confrontations from two perspectives. The first one (Revelation 12:4) took place before the beginning of the world and is first spoken of by the prophet Ezekiel. The second one is future (Revelation 12:7–9) and will take place in the middle of the Tribulation period.

Two important things happen as the result of this second battle that is directly related to our current discussion. The first one is the deadly wound of the Antichrist recorded in the third verse of the thirteenth chapter of Revelation. The second one is the casting out of Satan to the earth after being defeated by the archangel Michael. Some commentators point out that at this point, Satan indwells the slain body of the Antichrist (the eighth king) and explains how he is brought back to life (Revelation 13:3). This could be possible, especially in light of verse thirteen of chapter twelve. However, such a conclusion is based more on an assumption than actual biblical fact. Because there is so much happening at this point in time, I have chosen to use the illustration on the following page to help in our understanding of these events' progression.

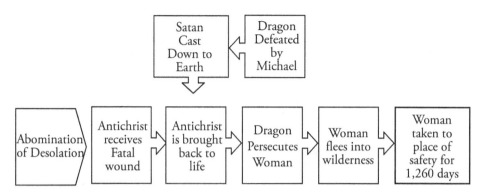

The point of all this is to draw attention to the fact that all these things takes place in the midpoint of the tribulation period which is identified either as 1,260 days (Revelation 12:6), forty-two months (Revelation 13:5), or "time, times, and half a time" (Revelation 12:14). The reasoning for giving days and months is to confirm the fact that 1,260 days is forty-two months of thirty days each or three and a half years. Remember, the time frame in Daniel, as is the case with John, is given from a Jewish perspective and not from our English calendar. It should be clear now that God provided these days and the events surrounding them to help us in our understanding of verses eleven and twelve of the twelfth chapter of the book of Daniel.

Although this was a drawn out discussion, it was necessary to bring the reader to the conclusion that the calculation of the 1,290 days mentioned in the eleventh verse of Daniel twelve starts from the middle of the seventieth week of Daniel; which in reality takes us thirty days beyond the tribulation period. The fact that all is not over at the end of the seventieth week is also supported by the fact the people leave the bodies of the two witnesses in the street for three days after their ministry is over (Revelation 11:7; cf. 11:3). As an aside, it should be pointed out here that this also shows the Bowl Judgments occurs sometimes during these seventy-five days and not during the seven-year tribulation period.

There remains one last thing to look at in explaining the extra forty-five days mentioned in verse thirteen of the twelfth chapter of Daniel. The only thing that is certain about this time frame is that it completes the seventy-five days that occur after the seventieth week. The angel does not expound on the blessing mentioned or who is included in it. The illustration below is provided as a means of understanding how these two times frames are to be seen in relationship to the seventieth week.

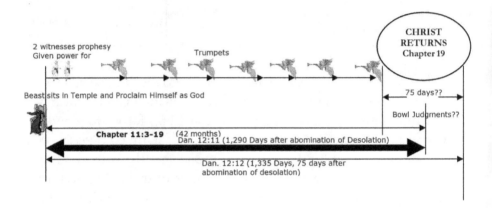

With all that will be happening during the last half of the seventieth week, one would think that man would run to God for forgiveness; however, this will not be the case. Instead, God still displays His mercy by sending three powerful angels to proclaim His Gospel throughout the world. We must not confuse the gospel proclaimed by these angels with that of salvation. Its content given to us in verse seven of the fourteen chapter of Revelation supports the view that it is not; instead, it is a warning to those still alive on earth against taking the mark of the beast. It is also a warning letting them know God is about to pour out the final plagues, or the bowl judgments out on the Beast, his kingdom, and all those who has accepted his mark. Someone might say at this point, "I thought the Gospel meant good news." To that comment, I would simply respond that it does mean good news, except in this case it is not that of salvation. Instead, it concerns God's mercy and compassion on those who have not taken the mark of the beast. When we read of the destruction that God will pour out on the Beast, his kingdom, and his followers, it becomes plain why this is regarded as good news.

The other major event that occurs during these seventy-five days will be the realization by the Antichrist that he has lost and lost big. As a result, he gathers all the armies of the world in the valley of Megiddo (or Armageddon), in preparation for the Battle of Armageddon (Revelation 16:14, 16). The carnage of this battle is beyond description. John does the best he can in trying to give us a picture of it. Birds (a reference to vultures perhaps) are called to eat the flesh of men whose blood rises as high as a horse's bridle is how John records the outcome of this battle (Revelation 19:18–19, 21). Whether he is being literal or figurative in his description is not the point. The purpose of the vision is to show that this will no doubt be a battle (if we can call it a battle, since the Lord simply speaks and it's over) like none the world has ever seen (Revelation 19:15). At the end, Jesus Christ will defeat the Antichrist and his armies. Obviously, God does not completely judge Satan at this time, but instead has him bound for a thousand years in the bottomless pit (Revelation 20:2–3).

There is no other place in Scripture that offers any stronger evidence the Lord's return occurs after the tribulation period than does Revelation eleven. While it's not possible to know the exact day, it is possible to determine the time frame. This is based on Scripture interpreting Scripture. When this principle is applied, no other conclusion can be drawn, other than the last trump spoken of in First Corinthians and First Thessalonians is the same one spoken of in the eleventh chapter of Revelation.

As stated earlier, the writer's aim is not to set dates, but to equip those Christians who will be alive during the last terrible days of the world. It is a means of preparing them for the calamities that will come on the world on the one hand, and give them the assurance and hope that God has not left them alone on the other. While we understand that it is the Holy Spirit alone who will ultimately strengthen the church, it must be understood that such strengthening only fully come when our knowledge of God's word is complete. Only then can we stand boldly and rejoice in the face of persecution and sorrow.

CHAPTER 16

BIBLICAL EVIDENCE FOR A PRE-TRIBULATION RAPTURE?

He who hath an ear, let him hear what
the Spirit says to the churches
—Revelation 3:22

Perhaps the most startling evidence given for a pre-Tribulation Rapture is the absence of the church in the book of Revelation after chapter three. Having spent many years studying and giving classes on the book of Revelation, I have honestly been unable to understand or find out where this belief came from. In this chapter, I will put forth passages occurring after chapter three of Revelation that clearly point to the church's presence in the world after the Antichrist rises to power. At the offset, let me say that I do agree that after chapter three, the word *church* does not appear again in Revelation until the final verses in chapter twenty-three (v.16).

However, when Pre-Tribulationists make this statement, the only question never asked is, "Is the term *church* the only word used to identify Christians in the New Testament?" There is no argument that its original meaning, "called out ones" (Gk. *Ekklesia*), aptly defines who Christians are. We have been called out of the world to be a people unto God in the same manner as the Jews were, that fact is unquestionable. However, when describing Christians in the New Testament, this term is seldom used. As we shall see in this chapter, there are many other terms and words used in the New Testament to describe Christians.

The first word or term that we want to consider (and perhaps most common) is *saint* (Gk. *hagio)*. Unlike *church*, it does not mean "to call out," but instead, "to set apart." Both words (*church* and *saints*) are equally important when identifying Christians, since by definition, the church consists of those who have first been set apart by God unto Himself. While it's true the church will always consist of wheat and tares (Matthew 13:24–30), this same statement is never true of the mystical church that comprises the body of Christ or the Universal Church. When writing to churches, Paul nearly always used this term in his greeting, especially when addressing serious matters about their spiritual condition (cf. Colossians 1:2; Philippians 1:1; Ephesians. 1:1). I believe he did this to perhaps draw attention to their position as saints—despite their conduct, it remains unchanged. Even the church at Corinth was still greeted in this manner, despite her spiritual deficiency (1 Corinthians 1:2).

With this being the case predominantly in the New Testament, we can authoritatively say the term *saint* is never used of unbelievers in the New Testament. In other words, when used in Scripture, this term always refers to the body of Christ. Unlike modern society, or even the society during the days of the apostles, it never refers to people who are good, or in some way have achieved a super level of spirituality by their own strength or deeds. Instead, it is a term applied to all Christians, regardless of their external appearance, character, merit, or behavior. In saying this, I am only stressing the writer's position and by no means implying or supporting the idea that one can sin as much as one wants, which is the teaching known as antinomianism. As Christians, we have a debt to live a life that is reflective of who we are positionally. We do this by constantly yielding to the Holy Spirit's guidance and teaching (Romans 6, 8:9–13).

With this in mind, let us examine some passages in the book of Revelation that occur after the fourth chapter, that make use of this term. In chapter thirteen, we find that, "it was given unto him [Antichrist] to make war with the saints, and to overcome them [saints]" (v. 7). Also in that same chapter, we read that "here is the patience and the faith of the saints" (v. 10). Based on these and other passages (Revelation. 14:12; 15:2; 16:6; 17:6), it becomes obvious there are saints on the earth during the reign of the Antichrist. Even those who argue that there's no real way of finding out what period of time is covered in these passages, must at least agree that it occurs sometime during the Tribulation period; since this is the only time the Antichrist's power will be of this caliber. Furthermore, the book of Daniel confirms the fact the Antichrist will wage such a campaign against Christians during this period (Daniel 7:21). Therefore, it's obvious the events described in the verses mentioned earlier happens after the start of the Tribulation and probably continue throughout the latter half (cf. Revelation 13:5), and perhaps all the way to the end of Daniel's Seventieth Week.

As discussed in a previous chapter, we cannot divide the body of Christ. This fact alone, if nothing else, must be considered when accepting the pre-Tribulation Rapture. This is especially true when Scripture is clear that saints are on earth during at least the last half of Daniel's Seventieth Week. If the church was raptured after the events in chapter four, yet there remain saints alive on earth according to the passages mentioned earlier, where did they come from and who are they? More importantly, how did they become part of the overall body identified in chapter seven of the book of Revelation (vv. 9, 13–14)?

Not only are the terms *church* and *saints* used to identify Christians; there are other phrases that are specific to Christians. I might point out some of these terms are recorded in the book of Revelation after chapter four. One such phrase is *remnant of her seed*, found in the twelfth chapter of Revelation (v. 17). It would seem inconceivable that anyone would apply this phrase to anyone other than Christians (Galatians. 3:28). I base this on the imagery in that passage combined with other supporting passages in the Old Testament. Also, a prophetic tone is seen in the figurative language of the woman escaping the Antichrist's wrath. At the midpoint of the Tribulation period, the Antichrist will attempt to destroy the entire nation of Israel (symbolized by the woman in chapter twelve), and according to Zechariah, he nearly does. However, God intervenes and saves a remnant of the physical nation and keeps them until the end of the Tribulation period.

Based on this, the identity of the remnant mentioned in the latter portion of the seventeenth verse of Revelation chapter twelve couldn't be a reference to the physical nation of Israel. It has to be someone else, someone who has an intimate relationship to the seed and not the nation. When looked at from this perspective, the only other group that qualifies is the church of Jesus Christ. Christians are linked to Israel in the sense that it was through her the Savior was born. He is the seed from which we are born into the spiritual house of Israel through the power of the Holy Spirit. Therefore, the remnant of the "seed" cannot be physical Israel, but those Christians living during the latter half of the Antichrist's reign.

In his letter to the church at Galatia, Paul addresses this issue in detail. In chapter three of that letter, he states that, "Now to Abraham and his seed were the promise made. He saith not, and to seeds, as of many; but as of one, and to thy seed" (v. 16). In other words, the physical nation of Israel descends from Abraham's seeds (that is Abraham Isaac and Jacob). They came to be by the direct result of God's supernatural work in the lives of Abraham and Sarah. But this promise found its fulfillment only partly in the birth of Isaac and subsequent birth of Jacob, whose name God changed to Israel. The promise that all nations of the world would be blessed through him (Genesis 12:3) was fulfilled not through his physical descendants but from the descendent, the seed—namely, Jesus Christ. He was and still is the only means by which the whole earth could be blessed. Paul alluded to this fact in his letter to the Romans by stating, "For he is not a Jew, which is one outwardly, neither is that circumcision, which is outward in the flesh: But he is a Jew, which is one inwardly; and circumcision is that of the heart, in the spirit, and not in the letter" (Romans 2:28–29 KJV). In making such a statement, Paul wanted his Jewish brothers to fully understand the true Jew (spiritually) is not those who have the physical circumcision, but those who have undergone a spiritual one. Therefore, the remnants being discussed in the twelfth chapter of Revelation must be seen from this perspective. In other words, the remnant rescued by God is the physical descendent of Abraham's seeds and those the Antichrist makes war with are the spiritual descendants of Abraham's seed. Illustration 1 further highlights this truth.

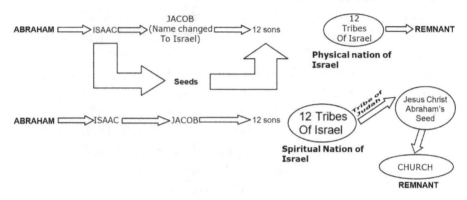

Illustration 1

What is evident here is that when we compare scripture with scripture, it becomes clear the remnant John refers to in Revelation chapter twelve has to be the church (spiritual Israel) and not the physical nation of Israel.

Another term used in the book of Revelation that is unique to Christians is the term *servant*. With the exception of *saint*, there is no other word used more frequently in the New Testament in identifying Christians. For example, Paul mentions it some seventeen times throughout his letters (cf. Romans 1:1; 14:4; 16:1; 1 Corinthians 7:21; 22; 9:19; Galatians 1:10; 4:1, 7, Philippians 2:7, Col. 4:12, 2 Timothy 2:24; Tit. 1:1, Philemon 16). Four times he uses it of himself (Romans 1:1; Gal. 1:10; Colossians 4:12; Titus 1:1). However, like most words in the New Testament, one could easily be misled into believing that a servant is anyone in the service of another. Although this is true in a general sense, it is not so when used of Christians.

The word *servant*, as used in the New Testament is translated from four different Greek words. They are *oiketes* (Luke 16:13; Romans 14:4; Philemon 16), *therapon* (cf. Hebrews 3:5), *diakonos* (Romans 13:4; 1 Corinthians 3:5), and *doulos* (Romans 1:1; Galatians 1:10; Colossians 4:12). The first term (*oiketes*) is used mainly of household servants or those who live in a house but are not part of the household, and are regarded as domestic workers. On the other hand, *therapon* is different. It does refer to a servant, but not a servant in a domestic sense. *Therapon* is the man who is more like a cherished friend of the master. He is the person the owner leaves to handle his affairs while he's away. Moses was this type of servant, faithful in all His (God) house as a *therapon.* In other words, God's house in this sense was the nation of Israel. God gave him the Law and His revelation, which were to be used in the administration of His people. As the cherished servant of God, he faithfully performed those duties given him while in God's house.

However, of all these terms, the one used in reference to Christians' relationship to Christ is *doulos*. A *doulos* is the man or woman who is in total servitude to their master. As such, his will is altogether wrapped up in doing those things that please his master. He subjects himself to his master, even to the point of disregarding his own life. Paul brings out this point in his letter to the Galatians in the phrase "nevertheless I live; yet not I, but Christ liveth in me" (Galatians 2:20). All Christians echo Paul's testimony that we are not our own because Christ has bought us from the slave market of Satan. Therefore, our attitude should always be that of a *doulos,* a slave of Christ. When you think about it, all men are doulos in the sense that all of humanity are either the slave of Jesus Christ or slaves to their sin nature.

The purpose of looking at the various words translated as servant in the Bible is to point to yet another instance or reference to the church in Revelation. For years, I was taught, believed, and subsequently taught others the 144,000 sealed Jews mention in Revelation seven were physical Israel. However, on closer study of that chapter, in particular the Greek word translated as servant (Revelation 7:3), I came to a different conclusion. The word translated as "servant" in that passage is *doulos.* Based on the previous discussion on the distinctions between the various Greek words used for servant, this word seems to be the most important. This is especially true when trying to determine contextually who is being addressed or eluded to. In nearly all the New Testament letters, the writer's most frequent identification of himself is seldom his title or name but that of the *"doulos* of Christ" (Romans 1:1; Galatians 1:10; Titus 1:1; James 1:1; 2 Peter 1:1; Jude 1). Not only is it used of the apostles; it is used of Christians as well (cf. Colossians 4:12; Revelation 1:1). The reason for pointing this out is not because it's not already known, but because I believe its use was intentional in Revelation seven. It is placed there with the specific idea of highlighting the point that those sealed in Revelation seven are not Jews, but Christians. This view will be discussed more fully in the next chapter. My intent here is to highlight the truth that the term servant is another word used for the church of Christ.

I have tried to shed light on the misconception that just because the word *church* does not appear after Revelation four does not of necessity mean that Christians have been removed from the world. It is not my purpose to downplay any specific group's understanding of this very difficult book and the Rapture. However, I do believe that when such statements are made, they should be qualified so information being passed on to the reader or student is clear enough to lead them to a conclusion supportable by all of Scripture and not just a few verses.

CHAPTER 17

THE 144,000 SERVANTS OF GOD

And I heard the number of them which were sealed: and
there were sealed an hundred and forty four thousand.
—Revelation 7:4

During the Tribulation period, God will raise up 144,000 witnesses who will evangelize the world. They will conduct revivals that will be unequaled in church history. Are these statements true? Are we to believe that these Christians will be able to successfully conduct revivals while persecution of an untold magnitude is being waged against them by the Antichrist? Scripture clearly teaches that he will have power to overcome the saints and wear them out according to Daniel. Based on this, martyrdom will be worldwide and on a level unrivaled in history. Combine these facts with the popular belief among most Pre-Tribulationists the Holy Spirit will be taken out of the world before this period makes any type of meaningful revival unlikely since all revivals are by His sovereign power.

During the early church age, persecution was extremely high; so high that worship had to be conducted in secrecy, just as it is done in many parts of the world today where Christianity is outlawed. During that time, the number of Christians did not increase dramatically, but their faith in Christ did. It shone brighter than ever as they willingly gave their life for their Savior. Persecution is never designed to grow the church, but to purge and purify it. Added to this is that even after all the plagues that will fall on man when the six seals are opened and the seven trumpets are blown, he still refuses to repent (Revelation 9:20–21; 16:9, 11).

This is an important point, because if these 144,000 Jews are saved during the Tribulation period, how did it happen? Did John misunderstand the visions or misquote what he heard? In other words, if no one repents after the seven seal judgments, how then are these 144,000 saved? Were they part of the Christians who were seemingly left behind to handle this important mission? If this is true, we have to infer that Paul's comments to the Christians at Thessalonica was obviously in error (1 Thessalonians 4:11–16). Also, if this select group of Christians is saved during the Tribulation period, what type of salvation is it, grace or law? If the pretribulation view of the Holy Spirit being removed at the Rapture holds true, then the only logical conclusion is that it is by law.

When it comes to salvation, the New Testament makes it clear the only means of salvation is by grace through faith in Jesus Christ as the result of the regenerative work of the Holy Spirit (John 3:5–8 cf. Ephesians 2:1, 5–9). It is His quickening power that awakens man's spiritual dead soul to the awareness of his utter sinfulness and need of a Savior. In stressing the necessity of the gospel to salvation, Paul states that it is the power of God unto salvation (Rom. 1:16). However, this power is not effectual without the Holy Spirit. Without His power, there can be no revival (Ephesians 2:1). Let me be clear in saying that I understand and fully accept God's sovereignty. He can save whomever He wants to, and can do it when and how He desires; the pagan city of Nineveh is a clear illustration of this (Jonah 3:9–10).

However at the heart of the matter here is, God has chosen to bring salvation to the human race through the regenerative power of His Spirit, only after the gospel message has been preached or given. Apart from this, there is no other means by which man can be revived; even Nineveh had to hear the Prophet. This is not only Paul, Peter, or John's teaching, but Christ's; the emphasis being, we're either all saved by grace alone, or lost and condemned by the Law. Faced with these facts, the only conclusion one can draw about these

144,000 is, not only must they already be saved, but the number itself is not meant to be taken in a literal sense.

When reading Revelation, one must never forget the importance of numbers. Each number has its own unique meaning. For example, seven is symbolic for perfection or completeness, three is for the Trinity, four for the four corners of the earth, six for imperfection or evil, and so forth. When either number is multiplied by itself, it adds infinity to its meaning. This can better be understood from the passage in Matthew eighteen when Peter asked Jesus how many times should he forgive his brother. Christ response was "I tell you, not seven times, but seven times seven" (Matthew 18:21). In other words, the number of times we are to forgive one another is limitless. Now take this same principle and apply it to the number 144,000 in Revelation seven. This number itself is the product of 12 x 12. Twelve symbolizes organized religion (spiritually) of the world. There are twelve tribes of Israel. From them, God chose to set up the religion of Judaism. However, their inability to meet and fulfill the requirements of the Law made it necessary for a New Covenant to be established. This New Covenant would be established and sealed by the blood of Jesus Christ, who would, in turn, choose twelve apostles and teach them the doctrine of God. Aided by the Holy Spirit, they would be given the charge and responsibility of laying the foundation for a different kind of religion—Christianity. Unlike Judaism, it is built on a relationship born not from without, but from within. It is this relationship that brings all men into one relationship with each other through the baptism of the Holy Spirit, so there is neither Jew nor Gentile, male or female, Black or White—we are all one in Christ. Together, we comprise a multitude no one can number, for we are Old and New Testament saints alike. This is the number John saw in Revelation seven. This is the 144,000 John is referring to, not just 12 x 12 literally, but 12 x 12 symbolically.

How are we to understand this? The answer lies in the list given to us in Revelation chapter seven. To properly interpret it, we must rely on other portions of Scripture. This is important because when this one passage of Scripture is taken alone, we become more susceptible to the possibility of error. This point is brought out by the apostle Peter in his second letter that "Knowing this first, that no prophecy of the Scripture is of any private interpretation." By "private" he means that prophecy must be taken in light of all other scripture that relates to it. That's why one cannot understand the New Testament without first understanding the Old. When we apply this principle to the 144,000, we can compare it with the list given in the forty-eighth chapter of Ezekiel where the portioning of Israel during the millennium kingdom is given. He lists the twelve tribes as follows: Dan, Asher, Naphtali, Manasseh, Ephraim, Reuben, Judah, Benjamin, Simeon, Issachar, Zebulun, and Gad. Clearly, this list is different from that given by John. As a matter of fact, John's list is also different from that in Genesis forty-nine as well. However, for the purpose of this discussion, we will restrict our comparison to Ezekiel's and John since theirs are the ones that deal specifically with future events. For ease of comparison, these lists have been placed side by side in the chart below.

Ezekiel	Revelation
Dan	Judah
Asher	Reuben
Naphtali	Gad
Manasseh	Asher
Ephraim	Naphtali
Reuben	Manasseh
Judah	Simeon
Simeon	Levi
Issachar	Issachar
Zebulun	Zebulun
Gad	Joseph
Benjamin	Benjamin

The tribes listed by Ezekiel represents the nation of Israel during the millennium kingdom or the period after the Battle of Armageddon. Now if the list given by God in Revelation seven also represents the literal nation of Israel, why would they be different, especially since their only difference is place and time? In other words, why would God give John a list inconsistent with that given to Ezekiel? I believe the reason is to show the pure state of the nation in the seventh chapter of Revelation. She is pure in the sense the twelve tribes are indicative of the whole or complete spiritual nation of Israel. This is an inference based on Revelation fourteen, where we see the same group of people, but this time they are identified as virgins (cf. 1 Corinthians 11:2). What's important about that scene is that they're standing on Mt. Zion with the Lamb, which is Jesus Christ our Lord.

Lastly, note the absence of Dan, the idolater, from the list in Revelation. He is omitted in Revelation because God would not include that which is an abomination (Deuteronomy 7:25) within the perfect body of His Son, Jesus Christ. However, He did do so in Ezekiel's list because it fulfills His promise to Abraham (Genesis 35:12) that his physical descendants would inherit the entire land of Canaan. For more than six thousand years, the Jews have waited for the reality of this promise. The futile attempts by the world to bring peace to the Middle East will always fall short because of their failure to understand the changeless covenant made by God with Abraham.

In light of all that's been said, what conclusions can be drawn about the 144,000 Jews in the seventh chapter of Revelation? First, there is no scriptural evidence that points to them as being set aside for evangelism. Verse one and three clearly points out the purpose for their sealing: it is to protect them from the plagues that will come on the world when the first six trumpets are blown. An illustration of this is seen in the plagues that fell on Egypt. The Egyptians were directly impacted by all ten plagues, yet the Israelites were protected, even though they were in the same geographic location (cf. Exodus 8:24; 9:4, 7, 26; 11:7; 12:13). I believe the same thing is happening here. The sealing is an act done by God to point out that these are His servants. As such, they are under His divine protection. To see anything other than this is to add an interpretation foreign to the text.

In conclusion, Scripture is silent about a worldwide revival before Jesus Christ's return. It does however tell us that in the last days, man's god will be the Antichrist (Revelation 13:3–4, 8). They will worship him and blaspheme God and blame Him for the calamities falling on the world (Revelation 16:21). Persecution will once again rock the church, causing those who are not saved to fall away in droves (Matthew 24:9–10; 2 Thessalonians 2:3; 1 Timothy 4:1–3). The only ray of hope for the world will be the message of the two witnesses in Jerusalem during the last three and a half years of the Great Tribulation. It is to them that God has given the task of speaking His words (Revelation 11:3–7). Their testimony will be the only means that God will use for evangelizing the world, not the 144,000 mentioned in Revelation eleven. Our testimony will be the blood shed for our faithfulness to our Lord. We have been given the treasures of heaven and therefore have the awesome responsibility of making known these truths to God's people, to ready their hearts for the final showdown between God and Satan. Who are the 144,000 slaves of God? It is the children of (spiritual) Israel who are from the seed of Abraham—Jesus Christ of Nazareth.

CHAPTER 18

THE CHRISTIAN'S "BLESSED HOPE"

And, behold, there came with the clouds of
heaven one like unto a son of man.

Hope is the anchor of our soul during times of storms. Its grip is so secure and sure that we need not fear of sinking into despair or desperation. Such hope is necessary in a world that is becoming increasingly hostile to Christ and those whom He has chosen and bought with His blood.

In writing to the Christians at Rome, Paul makes the point in the twenty-fourth verse of the eighth chapter that they (Christians) are saved not by hope, but in hope. He wanted to remind them that although they were undergoing intense persecution on behalf of their Savior, they would be able to endure it all because they were living in a realm governed by hope (Romans 1:8).

This teaching of Paul about hope brings out the basic principle that all people live in one of two realms or worlds—that of hope or hopelessness. The realm of hopelessness has nothing to offer man, either here or in eternity because it works under principles that are extreme opposites of God. Those that are part of this realm cannot see their need for God and His saving grace and mercy. Even though they speak of believing in God, the god they speak of and believe in is one made in their image and likeness. He is a god they can control, one who changes and is always loving, kind and good. The thought of a God of wrath and justice is foreign to their thinking. This explains why the unsaved live as if though they are accountable to themselves and themselves only.

The old saying that "we live, and then we die," aptly describes such an attitude and its outward expression of sexual immorality, murder, drunkenness, drug abuse, and all manner of evil. This is what hopelessness does—de-emphasizes the value of life and the need to live justly. After all, if this life is all there is, why not enjoy it to the hilt?

However, the realm of hope has as its controlling factor the peace of God undergirded by faith. Its citizens live a life of expectancy because they know that this life is not the end; there is a day of reward or punishment for deeds done in this life. But more importantly, they live knowing that one day, their blessed Savior will return for them. So as the trials, tribulations, and difficulties of this world confront us, we are not dismayed, because our inner being is being strengthened day by day.

The purpose of this book has been to examine scriptural passage about the Second Coming. In doing so, the writer's intent was not to give any specific date or time but simply provide the reader with scriptural evidence that point out certain events must take place before our Lord's return. While all may not agree with the writer's conclusion, one thing that can be agreed by all is, we look forward to the glorious appearing of our Lord through the eyes of faith.

It is fitting that this last chapter ends with faith because without it, hope is baseless. The Hebrew writer in his description of faith and hope in the first verse of the eleventh chapter of Hebrews bring out this fact. When this verse is closely examined, we discover that hope is among the fruits of faith.

But what does the writer of Hebrews mean by the phrase *faith is the substance* of hope. To answer this question, we need to look at the meaning of the word *substance* because it holds the key to understanding the relationship between hope and faith. The Greek word for *substance* is *hupostasis* (hoop-os-tas-is). It is a compound word from *stasis* meaning "to stand" and *hupo,* which means "under." Therefore, the word itself means "to stand under a foundation." Dr. Wuest summarizes the meaning of this word as speaking "of the ground on which one builds a hope" (Kenneth S. Wuest, *Wuest's Word Studies From the Greek New Testament for the English Reader, Vol. Two, Hebrews in the Greek New Testament, Part 2,* Wm. Eerdmans Publishing Company, 1973). From Dr. Wuest's summation of faith, we see the necessary role played by faith in hope. Without faith, it is impossible to have hope because, of necessity, it must be based on God's word illuminated by His Spirit! This is something that all Christians must not overlook—mainly that although God has given us this faith, its growth is dependent on both the indwelling Spirit and His word.

This is the key to its development and explains its essentiality to a hope that is solid, strong and unshakable. Again, quoting from Vincent's Word Study on the word *faith,* Wuest states, "Faith apprehends as a real fact what is not revealed to the senses. It rests on that fact, acts upon it, and is upheld by it in the face of all that seems to contradict it. Faith is real seeing" (Kenneth S. Wuest, *Wuest's Word Studies From the Greek New Testament for the English Reader, Vol. Two, Hebrews in the Greek New Testament, Part 2,* Wm. Eerdmans Publishing Company, 1973*).*

The relevance to all this, and I hope this book is to reemphasize the fact, that time is winding down, and soon our Lord will return for His church. However, before He does, we can expect to go through some hard and difficult times. It will be characterized by suffering, trials, tribulation, and persecution that are unimaginable. What is it that will keep us strong? It is a blessed hope built on a faith that assures us that no matter how bitter and hard the times may become, we can stand because of God's word and the promises within it—*Maranatha*!

ABOUT THE AUTHOR

John J Cobb is an ordained Baptist minister who serves as one of seven associate ministers of Shiloh Baptist Church of Waukegan. He resides in Hoffman Estates, Illinois, with his wife of over forty-eight years. John Cobb has two children, five grandchildren, and two great-grandchildren. He is a former writer for the National Baptist Convention USA Inc. Sunday School Publishing Board. He is a preacher, keynote and conference speaker, and workshop facilitator. He also published a second book, *From Death to Life, An Overview of the Foundational Doctrines of the Christian Faith* (2012), now on sale.